THOMAS HARDY AFTER FIFTY YEARS

By the same author
Thomas Hardy

THOMAS HARDY
AFTER FIFTY YEARS

Edited by Lance St. John Butler
Lecturer in English Studies
University of Stirling

Selection and editorial matter © Lance St. John Butler 1977
Chapter 1 © F. B. Pinion 1977. Chapter 2 © R. M. Rehder 1977.
Chapter 3 © John Fowles 1977. Chapter 4 © Robert Gittings 1977.
Chapter 5 © Michael Alexander 1977. Chapter 6 © T. R. M.
Creighton 1977. Chapter 7 © David Lodge 1977. Chapter 8 © Mark
Kinkead-Weekes 1977. Chapter 9 © Michael Irwin and Ian Gregor
1977. Chapter 10 © Lance St. John Butler 1977. Chapter 11 ©
F. E. Halliday 1977. Chapter 12 © R. C. Schweik 1977

First edition 1977
Reprinted 1978

Published by
THE MACMILLAN PRESS LTD
London and Basingstoke
Associated companies in Delhi
Dublin Hong Kong Johannesburg Lagos
Melbourne New York Singapore Tokyo

Printed in Great Britain by
BILLING & SONS LIMITED
Guildford, London and Worcester

British Library Cataloguing in Publication Data

Thomas Hardy after fifty years
1. Hardy, Thomas – Criticism and interpretation –
Addresses, essays, lectures
I. Butler, Lance St. John
823'.8   PR4754
ISBN 0-333-21487-0

IN MEMORIAM
G.A.L.B. (1913–66) and D.M.B. (1920–63)

Contents

Notes on the Contributors   ix

Introduction   *Lance St. John Butler*   xiii

1   The Ranging Vision   *F. B. Pinion*   1

2   The Form of Hardy's Novels   *R. M. Rehder*   13

3   Hardy and the Hag   *John Fowles*   28

4   The Improving Hand: the New Wessex Edition of Hardy's poems   *Robert Gittings*   43

5   Hardy Among the Poets   *Michael Alexander*   49

6   Some Thoughts on Hardy and Religion   *T. R. M. Creighton*   64

7   Thomas Hardy as a Cinematic Novelist   *David Lodge*   78

8   Lawrence on Hardy   *Mark Kinkead-Weekes*   90

9   Either Side of Wessex   *Michael Irwin and Ian Gregor*   104

10   How It Is for Thomas Hardy   *Lance St. John Butler*   116

11   Thomas Hardy: The Man in his Work   *F. E. Halliday*   126

12   Thomas Hardy: Fifty Years of Textual Scholarship   *R. C. Schweik*   135

Index   149

Notes on the Contributors

MICHAEL ALEXANDER is a Lecturer in the Department of English Studies at the University of Stirling. He is the author of *The Earliest English Poems* and *Beowulf*, verse translations of Old English poetry in the Penguin Classics series; also of a critical study of the poetry of Ezra Pound, to be published by Faber.

LANCE ST. JOHN BUTLER is a Lecturer in the Department of English Studies at the University of Stirling. He is the author of *Thomas Hardy*, a study published by Cambridge U.P. in 1978.

T. R. M. CREIGHTON is Senior Lecturer in English Literature in the University of Edinburgh. He has held university lectureships at Reading, Makerere and Leeds, and a Professorship at Fourah Bay. Before he settled in the country in Scotland he lived for many years in Wessex. He is the editor of *Poems of Thomas Hardy: A New Selection* (Macmillan, 1974).

JOHN FOWLES is a novelist and poet with several awards and some well-known publications to his name. These include *The Collector* (1963), *The Magus* (1966), *The French Lieutenant's Woman* (1969), *Poems* (1973) and *The Ebony Tower* (1974).

ROBERT GITTINGS is a poet and literary biographer. His *John Keats* won the W. H. Smith Award for 1969 and his *Young Thomas Hardy* the Christian Gauss Award of Phi Beta Kappa in 1975. His *Collected Poems* were published in 1976, and his book *The Older Hardy* appeared in 1978. In 1970 he received the C.B.E. and was made a Litt.D. at the University of Cambridge, where he was educated. He has been Visiting Professor to several universities in the U.S.A.

IAN GREGOR is Professor of Modern English Literature at the University of Kent. His work is mainly in nineteenth- and twentieth-century fiction. Publications include: (with Brian Nicholas) *The Moral and the Story* (1962); (with Mark Kinkead-Weekes) *William Golding: A Critical Study* (1967); *Matthew Arnold's 'Culture and Anarchy': A Critical Edition* (1970); *The Great Web: A study of Hardy's Major Fiction* (1974).

F. E. HALLIDAY, after taking his degree at Cambridge, taught at Cheltenham College, but after the war moved to St Ives in Cornwall to devote all his time to writing. Many of his books are about Shakespeare and his age, but among his most recent ones is *Thomas Hardy: His Life and Work* (1972).

MICHAEL IRWIN is Senior Lecturer in English at the University of Kent. Publications include *Henry Fielding: the Tentative Realist* and a novel, *Working Orders*.

MARK KINKEAD-WEEKES is Professor of English Literature and at present Pro Vice-Chancellor of the University of Kent at Canterbury. He is the author of books on William Golding (with Ian Gregor), and Samuel Richardson; and of articles on Swift, Defoe, Richardson, Jane Austen, the Brontës, Whitman, Kipling, Lawrence, Golding, and African and Caribbean Literature. He has edited selections of the poetry of Pope and of critical essays on *The Rainbow*; and is now engaged on a study of 'Lawrence at Work 1912–20'.

DAVID LODGE is Professor of Modern English Literature at the University of Birmingham. His principal works of criticism are *The Language of Fiction. The Novelist at the Crossroads* and *The Modes of Modern Writing* (1977). He has edited several critical anthologies and literary texts, including *The Woodlanders* in the New Wessex Edition of Hardy's novels. David Lodge is himself a novelist, and his novel *Changing Places* was awarded the Hawthornden Prize for 1975.

F. B. PINION, former Reader in English Studies and a Sub-Dean at the University of Sheffield, is the author of *A Hardy Companion, A Jane Austen Companion*, and *A Brontë Companion*. His latest publications are *A Commentary on the Poems of Thomas Hardy* (1976) and *Thomas Hardy: Art and Thought* (1977). With Evelyn Hardy he edited *One Rare Fair Woman* (Hardy's letters to Florence Henniker) in 1972. He is co-editor of *The Thomas Hardy Society Review*.

ROBERT M. REHDER is a poet whose work has appeared in a number of periodicals and anthologies. His contributions to Persian studies include 'The Unity of the Ghazals of Hafiz' (*Der Islam*, 1974), 'The Style of Jalal al-din Rumi' (*The Scholar and the Saint*, 1975) and translations in the Penguin *Anthology of Islamic Literature*. He is in the process of translating Hafiz for the Penguin Classics. He has written on Mallarmé and is working on a book about Wordsworth and the Beginnings of Modern Poetry. Robert Rehder is a Lecturer in the Department of English Studies at the University of Stirling.

ROBERT C. SCHWEIK is the author of *Hart Crane: A Descriptive Bibliography* and *English and American Literature: A Guide to*

Reference Materials. He is a member of the editorial board of *English Literature in Transition* and has published studies of Hardy, Browning, and Tennyson in a wide number of scholarly journals and collections of essays. He is at present Professor of English Literature at the State University of New York.

Introduction

Thomas Hardy died half a century ago, in 1928. This collection of essays attempts an assessment of Hardy's importance today, largely by indirect means. The contributors have not set themselves directly to answer the question 'What does Hardy seem like to us today?' Instead each contribution proposes a thesis or a number of ideas that take advantage of the benefits of hindsight. In some cases this is obvious: serious appreciation of the cinema is a post-war phenomenon and David Lodge looks at Hardy through the modern glasses this medium provides; the study and editing of Hardy's texts has progressed steadily in the last half-century and R. C. Schweik summarises the results of this work and points to the areas in which it is not yet complete. In other cases the hindsight is less obvious although it is always an informing presence: for instance, Hardy's fiction relies on and develops a certain 'form' which, clearly, is inherent in the novels and stories themselves, but Robert Rehder's study of this form relies implicitly on a broader view of literary form than was available either when the fiction was published or even in 1928; since that time there has been new literature and new criticism and, to look the other way, the very Sophocles to whom Dr Rehder refers is a subtly different animal from our grandparents' Sophocles. In another case a most instructive use of hindsight is made by John Fowles who, as a practising novelist, bridges the eighty years that have elapsed since the publication of *The Well-Beloved* with the long arch of his own identification with the psychological genesis of that most revealing novel.

These, and the other essays, give us the Hardy that exists so long after the man Hardy died. It is a different being, of course, because, like all great writers, Hardy has grown and changed since his death. This curious paradox of a sort of tenuous continuing post-mortem existence would not have greatly astonished him: one of the constant themes of his poetry is that people continue to exist after death for as long as they are remembered. Memory re-creates, forgetfulness destroys. The early poem 'Her Immortality' is an example. 'She' tells the poet:

> A Shade but in its mindful ones
> Has immortality;
> By living, me you keep alive,
> By dying you slay me.

By this logic Hardy is alive and with us, perhaps more alive today
than at any time since his death. The essays that follow go some way
towards answering the question of what aspects of Hardy predominate in this 'immortality'. At the very least they are evidence that
the 'second death', forgetfulness, has not overtaken him and that for
him, in a special way, after the first death there is no other.

Lance St. John Butler

1 The Ranging Vision

F. B. Pinion

To say that Hardy's style is not responsible for the steady growth of interest in his work would be specious; it can no more be dissociated from his imaginative thinking than form can be separated from expression in sculpture. His literary longevity owes much to his thoughtfulness and verbal economy, more to a creative gift which is often poetic, but most to his vision of life. Many of Hardy's poems are based on his own emotional experiences, and most of his stories are set in very circumscribed areas. Yet one does not think of him as egotistical or provincial. As an artist he has the rare faculty of combining imaginative experience relative to the individual (himself included) with an unwavering sense of man's place in the universe; his Wessex transcends topographical limits; and it is in wider dimensions that those elements which contribute most to his greatness are to be found.

Hardy's early poetic imagination was largely literary in origin, and the images he adopted tend to convey that sense of generality which made him feel their appropriateness to situations in his prose and poetry. Among them are gardens and the ravages of frost and blight, wintry severities, and the sufferings of birds. A superb early example is to be found in 'Neutral Tones'. He tells us that he knew little about love when he began to write poetry;[1] and yet, such was his imagination, he could write this and the 'She, to Him' sonnets. He was, I believe, looking far beyond the limitations of direct experience long before the essays of Arnold, Pater, and Leslie Stephen guided his reading and enlarged his critical independence.

Arnold's strictures on the provinciality of English writers are well known. In 'The Literary Influence of Academies' and 'The Function of Criticism' he charged them with egocentricity, quirkishness of style, lack of proportion, and lack of precision. Aeschylus, Sophocles, and Shakespeare had been fortunate to live in epochs of quickening ideas; the weakness of Byron and even Wordsworth was that, unlike Goethe, 'they had their source in a great movement of feeling, not in a great movement of mind'. He therefore stressed the role of the critic as a 'disinterested' seeker and disseminator of 'the best that is known and thought in the world'.

Whether Hardy's views differed significantly from Arnold's is dubious, though he declared that Arnold was 'wrong about provincialism':

> A certain provincialism is invaluable. It is of the essence of individuality, and is largely made up of that crude enthusiasm without which no great thoughts are thought, no great deeds done.[2]

One could wish Hardy had been more explicit. His 'crude enthusiasm' must be largely commensurate with that local appeal which commends elements of setting, character, or incident for artistic re-creation in accordance with the author's theme and vision of life. It is clear from 'The Profitable Reading of Fiction' that 'thoughts' cannot be dissociated from 'deeds'. They are creative and not extrinsic or didactic; they affect the course of action as well as the portrayal of character. A novel, Hardy says, is not 'the thing' but 'the view of the thing'; and 'characters, however they may differ, express mainly the author, his largeness of heart or otherwise, his culture, his insight, and very little of any other living person.' His standards of greatness may be judged by his definition of 'good fiction' as 'that kind of imaginative writing which lies nearest the epic, dramatic, or narrative masterpieces of the past', and by his reference to 'the old masters . . . from Aeschylus to Shakespeare'.

If a particular locality appeals to an author (Hardy or Jane Austen), however limited it may be, it can be adapted to imaginative settings and situations far more successfully than less familiar scenes. Wessex supplied quite enough 'human nature . . . for one man's literary purpose', Hardy wrote. Even though he derived a special satisfaction from preserving its old superstitious beliefs and customs, the artist in him was opposed to representative fidelity as a general rule. His subject was 'life' and not its 'garniture'. He thought he might be driven to write about 'social and fashionable life as other novelists did. Yet he took no interest in manners, but in the substance of life only.' He might have said with Wordsworth that 'the essential passions of the heart find a better soil in which they can attain their maturity' in rural life than in society. 'The domestic emotions have throbbed in Wessex nooks with as much intensity as in the palaces of Europe', he wrote in 1912, recalling, no doubt, his claim in *The Woodlanders* that, in a sequestered spot like Little Hintock, 'from time to time, dramas of a grandeur and unity truly Sophoclean are enacted in the real, by virtue of the concentrated passions and closely-knit interpendence of the lives therein'. His characters 'were meant to be typically and essentially those of any and every place where

> Thought's the slave of life, and life time's fool,

– beings in whose hearts and minds that which is apparently local should be really universal'.[3]

Arnold exaggerated the extent of English intellectual provincialism, and gloomily assumed that contemporary writers were doomed to 'die in the wilderness'. In his formative period Hardy was capable of finding (in Arnold's words) 'a current of ideas in the highest degree animating and nourishing to the creative power'. The new scientific philosophy gave a formidable cogency to Shelley's thought; and the task of the tragic writer was admirably enunciated by Pater.[4] There was, in fact, a considerable weight of 'scientific opinion' in the country for the discerning thinker, and in none was it more constructive than in J. S. Mill, whose new 'religion of humanity' was rooted in the Positivism of Auguste Comte. Hardy's ideas came from these and other sources; they confirmed a philosophy of chance as opposed to Providence, and underlined the need for altruism through co-operation and education. Mischance and pity are the key to his most serious work, and he showed that the conflict between natural law and social and other circumstantial factors is capable of a tragic view which is essentially similar to that of the Greeks, as Richard Le Gallienne confirms in his conclusion that *Jude the Obscure* is 'an indictment of much older and crueller laws than those relating to marriage, the laws of the universe. It is a Promethean indictment of that power, which, in Omar's words,

> with pitfall and with gin,
> Beset the path we were to wander in,

and to conceive it merely as a criticism of marriage is to miss its far more universal significance.'[5]

Unlike a certain Slade Professor of Fine Art at Cambridge, Hardy rarely lost his 'sense of relativity' – 'as if there were no cakes and ale in the world, or laughter and tears, or human misery beyond tears'.[6] Two contrasting visions co-existed in his mind: the individual is both the centre of his own world and an insignificant entity in the scientific dimensions of space and time. As *Two on a Tower* exemplifies, the individual must assume a greater importance from the human angle than the immensities of the universe. Hardy never forgot this viewpoint even when his subject was the fate of millions in *The Dynasts*; the duality of his vision is represented by the Spirit of the Pities and the Spirit of the Years. There is a reminder of it in the tragi-comedy of Jocelyn Pierston:

> How incomparably the immaterial dream dwarfed the grandest of substantial things, when here, between those three sublimities – the sky, the rock, and the ocean – the minute personality of this washer-girl filled his consciousness to its extremest boundary, and the stupendous inanimate scene shrank to a corner therein.

Particularly poignant is Sue Bridehead's heartfelt comment on Little Father Time: 'There's more for us to think about in that one little hungry heart than in all the stars of the sky.'[7]

The other view is inescapable. It comes to Knight in a flash of geological time as he hangs perilously on the Cliff without a Name. Whatever the sufferings of Mrs Yeobright, or Eustacia, or Clym, Egdon Heath remains 'a face on which time makes but little impression'. In *Desperate Remedies* and *Tess of the d'Urbervilles* the ephemerality of love is poetically translated into the glory of gnats quickly passing through the sunshine. 'Mary's birthday. She came into the world . . . and went out . . . and the world is just the same . . . not a ripple on the surface left', Hardy wrote on 23 December 1925, remembering his poem 'Just the Same'. The thought is inherent in 'Life and Death at Sunrise', and in what Bathsheba hears and sees when she wakes near the pestilential swamp after discovering the reach of Troy's perfidy.

A drab wintry view of Tess and Marian at Flintcomb-Ash reveals them as flies crawling over the landscape. The adverse 'circumstantial will' which determines their lot is not equated with the gods, but the reminder of *King Lear* ('As flies to wanton boys are we to the gods') is echoed in the Aeschylean reference to the President of the Immortals' ending his 'sport' with Tess when she is hanged. The tragic gravamen in the satirical ' "Justice" was done' is that victims of chance such as Tess have, as Swinburne stressed, but one life to live; it is 'her every and only chance'. The thought is found in the second 'She, to Him' sonnet of 1866, and repeated by the heroine of *Desperate Remedies* when her 'single opportunity of existence' appears to be wrecked.

Such perspectives are inseparable from natural law and the great web of cause-effect which spreads through the universe and society. Middleton Murry was right in affirming that Hardy's 'reaction to an episode has behind and within it a reaction to the universe',[8] and nowhere is this more dramatically and successfully conveyed than in the mythopoeic threshing scene, which symbolises Tess's suffering and gradual loss of will when driven by machinery kept in motion by 'the *primum mobile*' of her 'little world'. (The Prime Mover was synonymous with God in medieval philosophy, and equated with the First Cause by Positivists such as Hardy's friend Frederic Harrison.) Tess suffers in consequence of early misfortune at the hands of chance until she is desperate, and the tragic climax of her life is vividly anticipated in the flash of temper which makes her cry out, 'Once victim, always victim – that's the law!'

Local history extended the range of Hardy's vision of life. Around Dorchester he could not escape prehistoric burial-mounds and fortifications; Maumbury Ring and the discoveries of excavators reminded him of 'The power, the pride, the reach of perished Rome'; and aged country people still remembered defensive preparations against a Napoleonic invasion. His historical sense of proportion is seen in the aerial pictures of *The Dynasts*; a longer perspective still, in the Spirit of the Years. Human folly continues, and Hardy would not have ended *The Dynasts* as he did had he foreseen the 1914–18 war. He had met politicians, and was depressed to think how far a people's destiny depended on men of such limited views; for twenty years he had advocated a League of Nations. As nationalistic greed and public indifference made a second major war seem inevitable, he concluded that it was time to end 'visioning/The impossible within this universe';

> And if my vision range beyond
> The blinkered sight of souls in bond,
>   – By truth made free –
> I'll let all be,
> And show to no man what I see.[9]

Hardy's familiarity with the Bible probably did more to enlarge his historical sense than any other literature. He shares the psalmist's view that 'a thousand years' are but 'as yesterday', and sees the continuity of life ('seed-time and harvest shall not cease'), 'Though Dynasties pass'.[10] Biblical echoes are almost legion in Hardy's fiction, and where they refer to well-known events and figures (Cain and Job, for example) they still have a universalising effect. Their aptness is such that often, in a flash, they supply an imaginative release which confirms the immutability of human nature, as when, at the end of 'Old Mrs Chundle', the curate, stunned by the realisation of his false Church standards, goes out 'like Peter at cock-crow'. It is easy to miss the implications and aptness of Hardy's Biblical quotations. When Bathsheba looks at the white face of the coffined Fanny Robin, she fancies that it shows a consciousness of the retaliatory pain it inflicts 'with all the merciless rigour of the Mosaic law'. Only by studying the whole context of the quotation which follows (Exodus, xxi. 22–5) can one see how it applies to Troy (about to enter) as much as to Bathsheba.[11] Hardy's Biblical analogies seem least convincing where they are most ambitious: in the Jude-Jesus parallels which were dictated by his Christminster-Crucifixion theme.

Hardy achieves a considerable degree of universality through his use of literature. The major actions of *The Return of the Native* and *The Mayor of Casterbridge* are imagined within short distances from his birthplace. The perennial conflict between hedonistic selfishness and altruistic zeal in the former is adapted from Arnold and Pater, and heightened by Hardy's sense of natural defect in a Darwinian world. In the latter his immediate aim was a successful weekly serial with continual excitement and suspense. His main purpose was to please at a much higher level, and with this in view he drew Wessex parallels to the Old Testament story of Saul and David, to the *Oedipus Rex* of Sophocles, to *King Lear*, and even more notably to *Les Misérables*.[12] After experimenting in various directions, in long short stories and novels, he gives the impression of setting himself high tragic standards, and of aiming to enhance the imaginative appeal of his story through the creation of elements suggested by scenes which had proved their worth in various countries from ancient to modern times. Hardy is no mere borrower, however closely the final philosophy of Elizabeth-Jane resembles that which concludes Sophocles' play. He adapts and transmutes, and the critical question relates not to the means but to the result. Only a creative writer with imaginative vision can re-create effectively in this way, and only situations which are essentially the same throughout the ages can respond to this kind of treatment. The artistry of *Tess of the d'Urbervilles* cannot be fully appreciated without a realisation of its indebtedness in idea and imagery to Shakespeare's *The Rape of Lucrece* and Richardson's *Clarissa*.[13] I am not sure that any other English novelist has had a stronger traditional awareness of this kind than Hardy. 'It cannot be inherited,' writes T. S. Eliot, 'and if you want it you must obtain it by great labour' :

the historical sense involves a perception, not only of the pastness of the past, but of its presence; [it] compels a man to write not merely with his own generation in his bones, but with a feeling that the whole of the literature of Europe from Homer and within it the whole literature of his own country has a simultaneous existence and composes a simultaneous order.[14]

Readers familiar with *The Waste Land* will appreciate the generalising dimensions which literary quotations and allusions can give to the particular. Hardy's works are strewn with them from many sources, ancient and contemporary, English and foreign, as, for example, these from Shakespeare: the 'anguish that is sharper than a serpent's tooth' links the Marchioness of Stonehenge with Lear; 'his nature to extenuate nothing', Henchard with the noble bearing of Othello in adversity; 'the serpent hisses where the sweet birds sing', Tess and *The Rape of Lucrece*. A similar but more extended univer-salising effect is obtained by Hardy's association of his tempters with Goethe's Mephistopheles or Milton's Satan.

Two pastoral scenes with classical references have remarkable overtones. At Talbothays the declining sun casts shadows of the cows in the milking-sheds 'with as much care over each contour as if it had been the profile of a Court beauty on a palace wall; copied them as diligently as it had copied Olympian shapes on marble *façades* long ago, or the outline of Alexander, Caesar, and the Pharaohs'. This time perspective carries the same connotation as Shirley's

> The glories of our blood and state
> Are shadows, not substantial things.

After the shearing-supper in *Far from the Madding Crowd*, Jacob Smallbury 'volunteered a ballad as inclusive as that with which the worthy toper old Silenus amused on a similar occasion the swains Chromis and Mnasylus, and other jolly dogs of his day'. 'The sun went down in an ochreous mist', but the shearers 'talked on, and grew as merry as the gods in Homer's heaven'. Here, *inter alia*, we glimpse the continuity of essential occupations throughout the ages, and are reminded (incidentally) of a timelessness which Hardy's rustics often acquire from choice comments expressing the wit, wisdom, humour, and foolishness of the common people. They may derive something from Hardy's Wessex, more from his imagination; they are, as he says of the best fiction, 'more true . . . than history or nature can be'.[15]

The range of Hardy's vision is multiple, and the result is frequent, sometimes juxtaposed, changes of perspective. The classical associa-tions of the sheep-shearing supper have a rich imaginative effect, but more significant for the story than Smallbury's ballad is Bathsheba's singing of the verse 'For his bride a soldier sought her' in a traditional song. When the feverish Clym Yeobright, convinced that Eustacia is responsible for his mother's death, sets off to confront her at Alder-worth, we are reminded of the tragic expression of Oedipus; and almost immediately afterwards we are arrested by 'the imperturbable countenance of the heath, which, having defied the cataclysmal onsets of centuries, reduced to insignificance by its seamed and antique features the wildest turmoil of a single man'. Nothing expresses the artistic function of Egdon Heath more vividly than this image. Similarly, before the classical associations of Talbothays, we have a distant view of Tess in the flat pastoral valley, 'like a fly on a billiard-table of indefinite length, and of no more consequence to the surroundings than that fly'.

Hardy's vision ranges from the minute to the universal, from vernal leaves like new-spun silk to 'the full-starred heavens' of winter in 'Afterwards', from fern-sprouts 'like bishops' croziers' to the vari-coloured constellations over Norcombe Hill, and from Drummer Hodge, the unknown Wessex soldier, to the wonder excited by the 'strange-eyed constellations' which remain 'his stars eternally' in the southern hemisphere.

'In a Museum' and 'A Kiss' show Hardy's scientific imagination lost in wonder at sounds travelling from earth through space or starting from widely distant eras to mingle in 'the full-fugued song of the universe unending'. In 'According to the Mighty Working' he thinks of the web of cause-effect for ever woven throughout the universe by the Spinner of the Years. It is responsible for disasters such as the loss of the *Titanic* or the international tragedy of *The Dynasts*; for hereditary characteristics which determine so much in life ('Discouragement', 'The Pedigree'); and for strange physical transformations from death and burial ('Voices from Things Growing in a Churchyard').

Hardy's altruism extends to the whole living world, just as his patriotism applies to the whole globe regardless of race ('The Wind Blew Words'). In 'The Darkling Thrush' (influenced perhaps by Keats's 'What the Thrush Said')[16] and 'An August Midnight', he recognises that the humblest creatures may have insights beyond the reach of human senses and intellect. Waterloo makes him think not only of human carnage but of distress and destruction before the outbreak of battle, in birds and butterflies, animals above and below ground, flowers in bud, and unripened fruit and corn.

The general in the particular may be found in Hardy scenes relating to marriage. The woman of 'She Visits Alone the Church of Her Marriage' is any one of a countless number who have happy recollections of their wedding-services; the poem is a wonderful evocation of a common experience. The road which Henchard and his wife follow at the opening of *The Mayor of Casterbridge* is dusty and worn; by it a weak bird sings 'a trite old evening song' such as could have been heard there at the same time for centuries; the couple are strangely individualised but the staleness of their marriage is a commonplace of time. Unlike them, the pair in 'John and Jane' are generic; their parental expectations and experience are all too common. Even in 'She Hears the Storm', which is so specifically localised that the widow could be Hardy's mother (or grandmother), no attempt is made to reduce the general reference of the imagined experience.

Hardy can look at his own private sorrow in a detached way. His marriage proved to be very unhappy, and with hindsight he often regretted that he had not married this person or that (always assuming, it seems, that each would have married him). But for 'a stupid blunder of God Almighty' he would (he thought) have married Helen Paterson, the illustrator of *Far from the Madding Crowd*. His poem on the subject, 'The Opportunity', shows no self-pity; its jaunty measure proclaims a wry acceptance of a common plight, and the acknowledgement is more defined when it is seen that the form of the poem is based on Browning's 'Youth and Art', which has exactly the same theme.

Another Browning theme, that of 'The Statue and the Bust', becomes the subject of 'The Waiting Supper', a story which, like so many of Hardy's, shows the hold of boyhood memories. The original of the hissing waterfall which expresses the tragic irony of situation came to his notice when his father was employed by the architect Benjamin Ferrey in the rebuilding of Stafford House near Lower Bockhampton. Hardy felt impelled to use places connected with his forbears in his stories. In *Jude the Obscure* he was tempted to use the names of relatives at Fawley of whom he had heard from his grandmother; he abandoned them, but it was filial piety which determined the precise Marygreen setting of that novel, just as interest in three generations of Hardys suggested *Under the Greenwood Tree*, and his mother's childhood the setting for *The Woodlanders*. All these stories, ranging from the relatively idyllic to the tortured and tragic, enjoy a universality of appeal which transcends their Wessex topography. As the cramping effect of the Christian Church becomes more remote and unintelligible in the course of time, *Jude* may appear more 'provincial'.

One can have local attachments without having a provincial outlook. Hardy discovered in Italy that he had taken 'Dorchester and Wessex life' with him. At Fiesole the sight of an ancient coin reminded him of Roman remains unearthed in his grounds at Max Gate. In Venice he noticed that the bell of St Mark's campanile had 'exactly that tin-tray *timbre* given out by the bells of Longpuddle and Weatherbury, showing that they are of precisely the same-proportioned alloy'. His historical sense was assisted by his architectural knowledge. After a few days in Rome, 'its measureless layers of history' seemed 'to lie upon him like a physical weight'.[17] One reason he did not wish to visit the United States was that he preferred places with historical layers, and this interest is to be found in some of his more amusing poems such as 'Aquae Sulis', 'The Coronation', and 'Christmas in the Elgin Room'.

In 'After the Fair' Hardy sees the High Street of Casterbridge deserted at midnight by all but the ghosts of its buried citizens,

> From the latest far back to those old Roman hosts
>   Whose remains one yet sees.

The stories of *A Group of Noble Dames* have a basis in Wessex history, and we are asked to imagine their narration in the Dorset County Museum, where finally they assume their appropriate place in the long perspective of time, as 'a single pirouetting flame on the top of a single coal' makes 'the bones of the ichthyosaurus seem to leap, the stuffed birds to wink', and 'the varnished skulls of Vespasian's soldiery' to smile.

When Hardy concluded *Moments of Vision* with 'Afterwards' he did not expect to live much longer. Yet three more volumes of his poetry were to appear. The sundial design which he had used to illustrate 'The Temporary the All' aptly serves as an introduction to his poetry. It was clearly planned for the eastern turret of Max Gate, but not executed until after his death. From his study window he could see Conquer Barrow, a prehistoric mound, not far away. His poems show that he often thought of the dead he had known, and particularly of his wife, his parents, and his sister Mary, buried at Stinsford, across the valley. Near their burial-ground is Kingston Maurward, the manor house where, in his early boyhood, he had fallen in love with the lady whose ageing (imaginatively recalled in the tragic ending of *Two on a Tower*) shocked him unforgettably in later years. It is of her and fleeting time that he had thought in 'The Dream-Follower' :

> A dream of mine flew over the mead
>   To the halls where my old Love reigns;
> And it drew me on to follow its lead :
>   And I stood at her window-panes;
>
> And I saw but a thing of flesh and bone
>   Speeding to its cleft in the clay;
> And my dream was scared, and expired on a moan,
>   And I whitely hastened away.

A barrow is excavated on Bincombe Down, a few miles off, and he writes 'The Clasped Skeletons', recalling famous lovers in Hebrew, classical, and medieval history, and reflecting that they are but of yesterday compared with the fossils near the pair whose bones have recently been brought to light. In 'Evening Shadows' he thinks of shadows cast by Max Gate after his death, and how the shadow of Conquer Barrow is likely to outlast the Christendom which super-seded the pagan myths of the period when it was constructed. Implicit in the thought of 'Waiting Both' is the web of natural law which extends through stellar space and the individual; a star looks down and agrees with Hardy that they must each 'Wait, and let Time go by' until the inevitable change comes. Max Gate is 'The House of Silence', and the 'visioning powers' which he attributes to his 'phantom' self in the poem of that title are no exaggeration:

> 'It is a poet's bower,
> Through which there pass, in fleet arrays,
> Long teams of all the years and days,
> Of joys and sorrows, of earth and heaven,
> That meet mankind in its ages seven,
> An aion in an hour.'

Hardy's statements on fiction and poetry square with his finest achievements. The 'whole secret' of the former lies in an 'adjustment' to 'things eternal and universal'; 'a poet should express the emotion of all the ages and the thought of his own'.[18] Great art springs from an alliance between the local and the contemporary and those relatively timeless issues which remain essentially unchanged because they are true to life. Mythical interpretations of life and the universe have in the end become scientific, and the principal key to Hardy's continu-ing success as a writer is that he combines to an unusual degree a scientific vision of man's place in the universe with an artistic realisa-tion of the greatness in writing which has commanded assent through the ages. I have taken the humanitarianism of his imaginative appeal for granted. It is because Pater, in drawing a distinction between 'good art' and 'great art' stresses this aspect of literature, and implies what I have attempted to illustrate in Hardy, that his conclusion to 'Style' is particularly appropriate:

Given the conditions I have tried to explain as constituting good art; – then, if it be devoted further to the increase of men's happi-ness, to the redemption of the oppressed, or the enlargement of our sympathies with each other, or to such presentment of new or old truth about ourselves and our relation to the world as may ennoble us and fortify us in our sojourn here, . . . it will also be great art; if, over and above those qualities I summed up as mind and soul – that colour and mystic perfume, and that reasonable structure, it has something of the soul of humanity, and finds its logical, its architectural place, in the great structure of human life.

In the end one is left wondering whether heart, imagination, and intellect combined in Hardy to achieve what Arnold regarded as 'the element by which the modern spirit, if it would live right, has chiefly to live'. He defined this as 'the imaginative reason'; Pater, more precisely, as 'the imaginative intellect'.[19]

NOTES

1 'After Reading Psalms XXXIX, XL, etc.'
2 *Life*, pp. 146–7.
3 The quotations in this paragraph are from Hardy's general preface of 1912, *Life*, p. 104. 'The Profitable Reading of Fiction', the first chapter of *The Woodlanders*, and Wordsworth's preface to *Lyrical Ballads*.
4 See 'Winckelmann' and 'Conclusion' in Pater's Renaissance studies.
5 R. G. Cox (ed.), *Thomas Hardy, The Critical Heritage* (London and New York, 1970), pp. 277–8.
6 *Life*, p. 226.
7 The two quotations are from *The Well-Beloved*, II. viii and *Jude the Obscure*, v. iii.
8 *Aspects of Literature* (London, 1920), p. 130.
9 See the last two poems of *Winter Words*.
10 'In Time of "the Breaking of Nations" '.
11 *Far from the Madding Crowd*, Chapter xliii.
12 The influence of Arnold and Pater on *The Return of the Native* and the parallelism of *Les Misérables* and *The Mayor of Casterbridge* are discussed in F. B. Pinion, *Thomas Hardy: Art and Thought*, London and Lotowa, N.J., 1977
13 See the volume referred to in the previous note.
14 From 'Tradition and the Individual Talent' in *Selected Essays* (London, 1932), p. 14.
15 From 'The Profitable Reading of Fiction'.
16 See Keats's letter to J. H. Reynolds, 19 February 1818. The poem begins: 'O thou whose face hath felt the Winter's wind.'
17 'In the Old Theatre, Fiesole' and *Life*, pp. 188, 193.
18 *Life*, pp. 252, 386.
19 Arnold, 'Pagan and Medieval Religious Sentiment'; Pater, 'Winckelmann'.

2 The Form of Hardy's Novels

R. M. Rehder

Hardy was reticent about his novels. When Virginia Woolf called upon him, he refused to be drawn about his writing. 'He was not interested much in his novels, or in anybody's novels: took it all easily and naturally.' She tried to bring the talk around to his work, but he simply changed the subject. Through all the small talk she glimpsed that there was more to him and she was impressed: 'He seemed perfectly aware of everything; in no doubt or hesitation; having made up his mind; and being delivered of all his work, so that he was in no doubt about that either . . . There was not a trace anywhere of deference to editors, or respect for rank or extreme simplicity. What impressed me was his freedom, ease and vitality.'[1] The members of Queen's College, Oxford, when Hardy visited them in 1923 after being elected to an honorary fellowship, discovered to their surprise that he was 'interested in everything he saw, and cultured, but surely not much occupied with books: indeed almost all of us, his new colleagues, would have struck an impartial observer as far more *bookish* than the author of the Wessex novels . . .'

This same reticence appears in his work. There are scattered references, but, on the whole, not very much to show how he wrote his novels and how he thought about them. He mentions in his autobiography the apprenticeship he put himself through to become a poet, but there is a remarkable lack of references to the novels he read and an absence of many opinions by him on other novelists. He has left much more about the poets he admired than the novelists. We know that he was an omnivorous reader.

The young man who showed Hardy about Oxford in 1920 when he came to receive an honorary degree and see a production of *The Dynasts* was more astute than his guide in 1923. Charles Morgan speaks of 'his gentle plainness' and observes that in external things Hardy 'was deeply old-fashioned'. This discovery seems to have helped him to make his final judgement:

He was not simple; he had the formal subtlety peculiar to his own generation; there was something deliberately 'ordinary' in his demeanour which was a concealment of extraordinary fires – a method of self-protection common enough in my grandfather's generation, though rare now.

There are many who might have thought him unimpressive because he was content to be serious and determined to be un-spectacular . . . He was an artist, proud of his art, who yet made no parade of it; he was a traditionalist and, therefore, suspicious of fashion; he had that sort of melancholy, the absence of which in any man has always seemed to me to be a proclamation of blindness.

There was in him something timid as well as something fierce, as if the world had hurt him and he expected it to hurt him again. But what fascinated me above all was the contrast between the plainness, the quiet rigidity of his behaviour, and the passionate boldness of his mind . . .

A passage in Hardy's autobiography confirms that his self conceal-ment was a deliberate method of self-protection. It is a flash of anger from those extraordinary fires that illuminates for a moment the depth of Hardy's self-consciousness :

none of the society men who met him suspected from his simple manner the potentialities of observation that were in him. This unassertive air, unconsciously worn, served him as an invisible coat almost to uncanniness. At houses and clubs where he en-countered other writers and critics and world-practised readers of character, whose bearing towards him was often as towards one who did not reach their altitudes, he was seeing through them as though they were glass. He set down some cutting and satirical notes on their qualities and compass, but destroyed all of them, not wishing to leave behind him anything which could be deemed a gratuitous belittling of others.

Self-concealment is, of course, a form and involves the creation of character.

Two of Hardy's earliest memories show the awakening of his sense of form : that emotion can be hidden in art and that vivid perceptions demand to be accompanied by words. He says that :

He was of ecstatic temperament, extraordinarily sensitive to music, and among the endless jigs, hornpipes, reels, waltzes, and country-dances that his father played of an evening in his early married years, and to which the boy danced a *pas seul* in the middle of the room, there were three or four that always moved the child to tears, though he strenuously tried to hide them . . . This peculiarity in himself troubled the mind of 'Tommy' as he was called, and set him to wondering at a phenomenon to which he ventured not to confess. He used to say in later life that . . . he danced on at these times to conceal his weeping. He was not over four years of age at this date.

This shows he was distrustful, as a young child, of spontaneous and strong emotion, pondering it as a problem. His response to this trouble is secrecy. 'In those days the staircase at Bockhampton (later removed) had its walls coloured Venetian red by his father, and was so situated that the evening sun shone into it, adding to its colour a great intensity for a quarter of an hour or more. Tommy used to wait for this chromatic effect, and sitting alone there, would recite to himself "And now another day is gone" from Dr Watts's Hymns, with great fervency, though perhaps not for any religious reason, but from a sense that the scene suited the lines.' The evening light on the red wall has neither a shape nor an intrinsic meaning, although it is the death of the sun and the end of the day. The effect is chromatic and Hardy is alone. He responds with words to a formless intensity. These are the sources of form.

Hardy rejected the idea that the novel should be merely a repre-sentation of sensation or the world. He shared with Henry James the belief that the art of the novel depends on selection and treatment. Thinking about 'the recent school of novel-writers', he wrote (15 September 1913): 'They forget in their insistence on life, and nothing but life, in a plain slice, that a story *must be worth the telling*, that a good deal of life is not worth any such thing. and that they must not occupy a reader's time with what he can get at first hand any-where around him.' The lost letters, missed trains and unexpected encounters in his novels are part of his effort to keep the story going. They are also ways of holding the story together as tightly as possible. Hardy prefers the definite. Like Shakespeare, like all great poets, he has a metaphor-making mind. He is less discursive than George Eliot and more specific than Henry James. Their tendency is to expand, his instinct is to concentrate. The terse, twisted quality of his prose shows the marks of this pressure. As the descriptions focus on details and each becomes a nexus of metaphors, the plots of the novels seem to crystallise around a sequence of small, individual, closed scenes. *Far from the Madding Crowd* can almost be described as a series of images. Hardy does not seek to create space in his novels, but rather to fill it. He has a need to make things happen, while Eliot and James have the ability to contemplate a mood by itself and often prolong their delays.

Hardy emphasises the importance of strict, rigorous form. He was delighted when the *Saturday Review* praised *A Pair of Blue Eyes* as 'the most artistically constructed of the novels of its time – a quality which . . . would carry little recommendation in these days of loose construction and indifference to organic homogeneity.' Writing about *The Famous Tragedy of the Queen of Cornwall*, he is at pains to point out that

> The unities are strictly preserved, whatever virtue there may be in that. (I, myself, am old-fashioned enough to think there *is* a virtue in it, if it can be done without artificiality. The only other case I remember attempting it in was *The Return of the Native*.)

Hardy told Gosse that his review of *Jude the Obscure* 'is the most discriminating that has yet appeared. It required an artist to see that the plot is almost geometrically constructed – I ought not to say constructed, for beyond a certain point, the characters necessitated it, and I simply let it come.' And in another letter he makes it clear that he thought of the novel as a balance of opposites.

When Hardy was unable to attend a dinner in London to honour Anatole France, he sent his regrets :

> In these days when the literature of narrative and verse seems to be losing its qualities as an art, and to be assuming a structureless and conglomerate character, it is a privilege that we should have come into our midst a writer who is faithful to the principles that make for permanence, who never forgets the value of organic form and symmetry, the force of reserve, and the emphasis of understatement . . .

He declared that he had abandoned writing novels 'with all the less reluctance' because the novel was 'gradually losing artistic form, with a beginning, middle, and end, and becoming a spasmodic inventory of items, which has nothing to do with art.'

From these statements (and there are others as well), it is obvious that Hardy had a carefully considered working definition of form. He stresses symmetry and tightness. He deplores the spasmodic, the heterogeneous and the conglomerate. By organic form he appears to mean that each story has its own form and that a novel should be all of a piece. He intimates that the protagonists make their own plot, that each character is a plot. The one critic who looms up in all this is Aristotle. This is certainly because of Hardy's preoccupation with tragedy.

Most of Hardy's novels have markedly unhappy endings. This is a significant characteristic of their form. He is the first major English author to write a number of novels that end unhappily, although the conclusions of his best novels can only be called tragic. He does not simply negate happiness, he insists on sorrow. His achievement, in terms of form, is to have combined the tragedy and the novel.

Hardy is a writer of great subtlety. He makes full use of 'the force of reserve, and the emphasis of understatement', but he can be obvious, heavy-handed and unrelenting as well. He seems sometimes to resemble the man with the tin pot of red paint in *Tess of the d'Urbervilles* who paints Biblical texts in fiery letters around the countryside, but he, nevertheless, continues to surprise us by the fineness of his observations, as when he describes how the strangers drinking outside Rolliver's inn 'threw the dregs on the dusty ground to the pattern of Polynesia', or Clym tying Eustacia's bonnet strings after their quarrel. He uses the most delicate touch and the hammer-blow. His harshness and his ruthlessness can obscure for us the fact that these qualities exist together. To understand this combination in Hardy's work, and its relation to his need of tragedy, it is necessary to look more closely at the novels.

The most dramatic moment in *A Pair of Blue Eyes* is when Knight hangs on the edge of the cliff above the sea. Hardy skilfully draws it out page after page. It is a moment of pure emotion, of extreme tension, fear and suppressed panic. Suddenly :

By one of those familiar conjunctions of things wherewith the inanimate world baits the mind of man when he pauses in moments of suspense, opposite Knight's eyes was an imbedded fossil, standing forth in low relief from the rock. It was a creature with eyes. The eyes, dead and turned to stone, were even now regarding him. It was one of the early crustaceans called Trilobites. Separated by millions of years in their lives, Knight and this underling seemed to have met in their place of death. It was the single instance within reach of his vision of anything that had ever been alive and had had a body to save, as he himself had now.

The creature represented but a low type of animal existence, for never in their vernal years had the plains indicated by those numberless slaty layers been traversed by an intelligence worthy of the name. Zoophytes, mollusca, shell-fish, were the highest developments of those ancient dates. The immense lapses of time each formation represented had known nothing of the dignity of man. They were grand times, but they were mean times too, and mean were their relics. He was to be with the small in his death . . .

'Time closed up like a fan before him. He saw himself at one extremity of the years, face to face with the beginning and all the intermediate centuries simultaneously.' Images of prehistoric men 'rose from the rock, like the phantoms before the doomed Macbeth', and then Knight has a vision of the animals that existed before man going backwards toward the trilobite.

This moment is unexpected. It is neither predicted nor prepared for by the narrative, and is not, of itself, necessary to the plot. Similarly, within the moment, the encounter with the trilobite is unexpected and presented as a coincidence, 'one of those familiar conjunctions'. Hardy is a master of such surprises. They are essential to his way of telling a story and to his understanding of the world. The two things are, of course, connected. The form of his under-standing is the form of his novels. He labours especially to try to say what everything means. His extensive use of coincidences is part of his effort to connect disparate events. How things happen is a con-stant problem for him. Often he seems to feel himself in a universe of unrelated accidents. Unable to find a cause, but feeling the need of one, Hardy will interpret an event by evoking the past or by substituting a metaphor for a cause. Here a man in pursuit of his hat slips on the brink of a precipice. Through images of prehistoric life, the accident is charged with the significance of the entire past and of every man's struggle to survive.

Knight's own life does not pass before his eyes, but the history of all life and time itself. Knight is fighting for his life. On the verge of falling to his death on the rocks below, he imagines life developing from the rock into man. It is as if he is trying to be born again.

The passage is remarkable for its representation of intense feeling. Amorphous, desperate emotion is contained by the precise, lasting shape of the trilobite. The major emotion of Hardy's poems is of a man haunted by his past. The poems are full of ghosts. The trilobite is a fossilised ghost and looks at Knight with its dead eyes. The ancient men appear 'like the phantoms before the doomed Macbeth'. This reference to Macbeth is a characteristic Hardy touch. Of a slightly different order from the other elements in the passage, it thereby opens up the description, and adds a hint of personal guilt, and of the dangers of fantasy. Fantasy – and all feeling – because it is threaten-ing, must be confined. The rush of fear becomes the fossil record. Science in Hardy's work has the emotional value of form. This suggests why there is so much science deliberately included in his narratives and why some of his most emotional stories contain so much rigid and scientific theory.

The description of the most indefinite and intangible seems to demand the mention of the most definite and tangible. The soft is balanced by the hard. There is a basic juxtaposition of animate and inanimate. Throughout Hardy's work there are many examples of emotion being described in this way. To see this is a prerequisite to appreciating Hardy's sense of form.

When Cytherea, in Hardy's first published novel, *Desperate Remedies*, discovers the secret love of Miss Aldclyffe, she thinks: 'Was this the woman of his wild and unquenchable early love? . . . Surely it was. And if so, here was the tangible outcrop of a romantic and hidden stratum of the past hitherto seen only in her imagination . . .' The geologic metaphor is used for Miss Aldclyffe's underground life and for 'wild and unquenchable emotion'. The notion of diffuse and powerful emotion as existing inside a container is explicit in another description of Miss Aldclyffe – 'The maiden's mere touch seemed to discharge the pent-up regret of the lady as if she had been a jar of electricity.' – and in one of Manston: 'Whatever were Manston's real feelings towards the lady who had received his explanation in these supercilious tones, they remained locked within him as within a cabinet of steel.'

Hardy imagines being in terms of surface and core. In *The Hand of Ethelberta*, Ethelberta defines the character of Neigh in these terms: 'She had set him down to be a man whose external inexcitability owed nothing to self-repression, but stood as the natural surface of the mass within.' The surface is consciousness and self-repression is self-control.

When Ethelberta begins her career as a story-teller she learns her power of creating a mask for her feelings:

It was in performing this feat that Ethelberta seemed first to discover in herself the full power of that self-command which further onward in her career more and more impressed her as a singular possession, until at last she was tempted to make of it many fantastic uses, leading to results that affected more households than her own. A talent for demureness under difficulties without the cold-bloodedness which renders such a bearing natural and easy, a face and hand reigning unmoved outside a heart by nature turbulent as a wave, is a constitutional arrangement much to be desired by people in general; yet, had Ethelberta been framed with less of that gift in her, her life might have been more comfortable as an experience, and brighter as an example, though perhaps duller as a story.

That Hardy sees this as generating his story is important. This is a clear illustration of how his way of thinking about feeling not only shapes characters and produces a style of description, but results in the creation of larger forms, including whole novels. The difficulty of communication is at the centre of his stories and the breakdown

B

of communication frequently leads to tragedy. This is symbolised by the notes and letters that continuously go astray, promoting catastrophe. It is the communication of feeling that is especially difficult. Characters are often isolated by their emotions, emotions that they can neither express nor explain – even to themselves. Ethelberta is never able to speak of her true feelings. Clym and Eustacia, Angel and Tess, are only briefly in touch with each other.

The face of Clym Yeobright in *The Return of the Native* reveals his consciousness. Again it is a matter of surface:

> But it was really one of those faces which convey less the idea of so many years as its age than of so much experience as its store. . . . The face was well shaped, even excellently. But the mind within was beginning to use it as a mere waste tablet whereon to trace its idiosyncrasies as they developed themselves. The beauty here visible would in no long time be ruthlessly overrun by its parasite, thought . . . But an inner strenuousness was preying upon an outer symmetry. . . .

George Somerset in *A Laodicean* is cast in the same mould. He, too, does not look as young as he is, 'owing to a too dominant speculative activity in him, which, while it had preserved the emotional side of his constitution, and with it the significant flexuousness of mouth and chin, had played upon his forehead and temples till, at weary moments, they exhibited some traces of being exercised.' If emotion cannot be mastered, it must be concealed: 'he possessed a moustache all-sufficient to hide the subtleties of his mouth, which could thus be tremulous at tender moments without provoking inconvenient criticism.' It must be noted that Yeobright becomes a preacher and devotes his life to attempts at communication, while Somerset 'preserved the emotional side of his constitution' through his 'dominant speculative activity'.

As feeling is *flexuousness*, control is commonly thought of in terms of stone. Ethelberta ceases to communicate and is virtually turned to stone: 'She had at this juncture entered upon that Sphinx-like stage of existence in which, contrary to her earlier manner, she signified to no one of her ways, plans, or sensations, and spoke little on any subject at all. There were occasional smiles now which came only from the face, and speeches from the lips merely.'

A more interesting example, because the metaphor is more likely to have been unconscious, can be found in *The Return of the Native*, immediately before the first love scene in which Clym and Eustacia speak to each other. Clym walks in the evening to Rainbarrow to watch the eclipse of the moon. He flings himself down in the heather to wait for Eustacia. As he lies there, he looks at the moon and his mind wanders.

> More than ever he longed to be in some world where personal ambition was not the only recognized form of progress – such, perhaps, as might have been the case at some time or other in the silvery globe then shining upon him. His eye travelled over the length and breadth of that distant country – over the Bay of Rainbows, the sombre Sea of Crises, the Ocean of Storms, the Lake of Dreams, the vast Walled Plains, and the wondrous Ring Mountains – till he almost felt himself to be voyaging bodily through its wild scenes, standing on its hollow hills, traversing its deserts, descending its vales and old sea bottoms, or mounting to the edges of its craters.

He longs for another world and is transported out of himself in fantasy. Moonlight is an old metaphor for the imagination, but Hardy enumerates the topographic features of the moon. Clym drifts away, Hardy maps the hard, rough surface. This vivid, but otherwise amorphous moment of self-abandonment is presented in terms of the moon's geology.

For many of Hardy's characters self-abandonment is formlessness and the self is a form that must be maintained by constant thought, a grip that cannot be relaxed. In the novel, Clym, who returns from the diamond business and of whom his mother says 'he can be hard as steel', is set against Eustacia, who has no inner strength and who is overpowered by the chaos of her feelings. Her emotions destroy her.

The crucial rejection of Tess by Angel in *Tess of the d'Urbervilles* is explained by his unfeeling hardness :

> She broke into sobs, and turned her back to him. It would almost have won round any man but Angel Clare. Within the remote depths of his constitution, so gentle and affectionate as he was in general, there lay hidden a hard logical deposit, like a vein of metal in a soft loam, which turned the edge of everything that attempted to traverse it. It had blocked his acceptance of the Church; it blocked his acceptance of Tess.

Tess is another heroine destroyed by her feelings. She is to Angel as Eustacia is to Clym. Perhaps it is her capacity for feeling that causes Hardy twice to juxtapose her and a machine (in Chapters 14 and 47). Certainly Hardy, with a sure sense of form, deliberately places her arrest and the penultimate scene of the novel in Stonehenge. Tess is seen sleeping, lying unconscious on a stone, and surrounded by a circle of stones. For Hardy Stonehenge is a place of human sacrifice and he wants a reference to the dawn of history to conclude his narrative of primitive emotion, guilt and sorrow.[2] Tess's history is felt to be incomplete without relating it directly to all human history. The stone stands for that which is most ancient.

The Well-Beloved is the last novel that Hardy published. Of all his novels it is the one that is most completely fantasy, as Hardy recognised: 'As for the story itself, it may be worth while to remark that, differing from all or most others of the series in that the interest aimed at is of an ideal or subjective nature, and frankly fantastic, verisimilitude in the sequence of the events has been subordinated to the said aim.' This history of an emotion in which reality is subordinated to fantasy is full of stone. The setting is the Isle of the Slingers, a 'peninsula carved by Time out of a single stone', 'a solid and single block of limestone four miles long', the 'Gibraltar of Wessex'. The inhabitants live in houses that are 'all stone, not only in walls, but in window-frames, roof, chimneys, fence, stile, pig-sty and stable, almost door', and most of them live by quarrying the rock on which they live.

The hero, Jocelyn Pierston, is the son of a stone-merchant and a sculptor. He is unable to love any one woman, but instead loves the fantasy of a woman, the Well-Beloved, that moves from woman to woman. He succeeds as a sculptor by attempting to cut 'his dream-figures' out of stone. His struggle is to realise his feeling: 'Jocelyn threw into plastic creations that ever-bubbling spring of emotion which, without some conduit into space, will surge upwards and ruin all but the greatest men.' He is a haunted man, and at one point, looks into a mirror and sees himself as a ghost. Because the life of his mind is given to feeling, not thought, he looks younger than he is, unlike Clym Yeobright and George Somerset, although at the end one of his loves sees him as 'a strange fossilised relic in human form'.

Form is never merely a container. It is always part of the meaning of a work and of the same substance. The nature of the shape itself, a response to hidden pressures, has a significance, even if we cannot decipher it.

Hardy's attitude to form as embodied in these descriptions shows how his self-concealment worked itself out in his fiction and how he thinks of form as a way of holding feeling. Sensation, potent, mysterious and Protean, seems at odds with everything solid and definite, but form is itself a feeling and allows more feeling. The shell enables the kernel to grow. Hardy's plots, his conception of character and his notions of development all come from this same matrix.

Wallace Stevens says of William Carlos Williams that, 'His passion for the anti-poetic is a blood-passion and not a passion of the inkpot. The anti-poetic is his spirit's cure. He needs it as a naked man needs shelter or as an animal needs salt. To a man with a sentimental side the anti-poetic is that truth, that reality to which all of us are forever fleeing.'[3] Hardy needs the tragic because of the overwhelming power of his feelings. It may be said that the novel as he found it was too slack and diffuse for his purposes. Tragedy may be considered the most rigorous of narrative forms, the novel is perhaps the most commodious. Hardy's combination of the two enables him to express sorrow as no other English novelist can. His work is remarkable for the varieties and nuances of sadness. Among English writers, perhaps only Shakespeare surpasses him in this capacity.

Hardy worked consciously and deliberately as an artist in the tradition of the greatest European art. His idea of tragedy represents a combination of Greek, Shakespearian and Biblical tragedy. He had Jesus and Paul in mind when he created Clym Yeobright. He found much of the form of *The Mayor of Casterbridge* in the histories of Saul and King Lear, and *Jude the Obscure* is reminiscent of Job. The customers in Warren's Malthouse, the old men in the Three Mariners and the people at Rolliver's perform some of the functions of a Greek chorus, as do many of the groups of folk in Hardy's novels. They are used to balance the novels. The way in which they are separated from, and contrasted with, the other characters is Shakespearian and derives from the ancient division between high and low styles.[4]

George Eliot told R. C. Jebb that Sophocles had influenced her most by his 'delineation of the great primitive emotions'.[5] This, I believe, also attracted Hardy to Greek tragedy. He is indebted to Aeschylus and Euripides as well as Sophocles. His sense of doom and of the momentum of tragedy is Greek. The bleakness of his view is matched by that of his great contemporary, Freud, another close student of Greek and Shakespearian tragedy, and the bleakness of both views is founded on a consideration of human sexuality.

For Shakespeare, tragedies end in death, comedies end in marriage. For Hardy, some tragedies begin in marriage and every comedy contains a tragedy. He agrees with Ruskin's remark 'that comedy is tragedy if you only look deep enough', and when he revised *Under the Greenwood Tree*, the novel that most resembles a Shakespearian comedy, he was aware of its possibilities for sorrow: 'But circumstances would have rendered any aim at a deeper, more essential, more transcendent handling unadvisable at the date of writing . . .'

Hardy wants always to go deeper and he is prepared to face anything. Shakespeare merges the forms of tragedy and comedy in order to explore morally ambiguous situations and the world of his imagination. Hardy follows him in an attempt to give a more complete view of ordinary life.

Hardy was a well-educated man, in a way that Dickens, Trollope and James were not. It is not surprising to find him on close terms with Leslie Stephen. He is an Eminent Victorian in the class of Arnold, Marx and Kierkegaard.[6] He is a thinker as George Eliot is a thinker, but as a learned writer with a highly developed literary sense of form, he is perhaps closer to Joyce, Gide and Mann. The exploitation of ideas in his novels suggests *Der Zauberberg* and *Doktor Faustus*, *Les Caves du Vatican*, *L'Etranger* and *La Peste*. He read *A l'ombre des jeunes filles en fleur* in 1926 and felt that Proust was developing further the subject of *The Well-Beloved*.

The way Hardy ends his stories, it is as if all his fantasies must be sacrificed to malignant, inner gods, as if nothing of the inner world should be allowed to endure. The dreamer is punished by having the dream destroyed. The catastrophes break the connection between the story and reality, and the story comes to an end. The awareness of death marks the return to time. Hardy returns in all his work to the thought of death. His alleged pessimism is no more than his vivid consciousness that every life ends in death and that death is final, and his inability to believe that there can be any reparation, not even symbolically, for most suffering and pain. He writes of death as a man who feels the full force of the 'unquenchable expectation' of the self: 'There is in us an unquenchable expectation, which at the gloomiest time persists in inferring that because we are *ourselves*, there must be a special future in store for us, though our nature and antecedents to the remotest particular have been common to thousands.'[7] Hardy's endings are a rejection of sentiment. He dwells on the worst as if to propitiate the future and to avoid the intolerable.

The tragedy in Hardy's novels is often the end of a dream. The awakening is a prelude to destruction, as if knowledge is forbidden. The characters are set against the nature of things, the entire universe, as in the Greek tragedies, and knowledge comes with the force of a blow. Will Strong, the hero of *The Poor Man and the Lady*, Hardy's first novel that was never published, was at one point in the story's history to become temporarily blind from too much study.[8] Clym Yeobright almost loses his sight in the pursuit of knowledge and never fully recovers it, and Hardy makes a number of references to the blindness of Samson. As Hardy wrote: 'The Scheme of Things is, indeed, incomprehensible; and there I suppose we must leave it — perhaps for the best. Knowledge might be terrible.' There seems to be an ambivalence here. He relates his stories as if the world had no meaning and yet feels the threat of some terrible mystery.

Charles Morgan speaks of Hardy's melancholy and suggests that it was the condition of his intelligence. Thought seems with him almost an act of mourning. Hardy was able to take into himself the vastness and the emptiness of the world. This meant coming to terms with his inner world. Discussing the writing of fiction, he speaks of the impossibility of 'reproducing in its entirety the phantasmagoria of experience.'[9] 'Phantasmagoria' shows that he is looking inward. He describes Casterbridge as 'a dream place'. Egdon Heath in a storm is the landscape of a dream:

> Then it became the home of strange phantoms; and it was found to be the hitherto unrecognized original of those wild regions of obscurity which are vaguely felt to be encompassing us about in midnight dreams of flight and disaster, and are never thought of after the dream till revived by scenes like this.

Most of the stories begin by watching an isolated figure or pair of figures moving in a vast landscape, often at twilight, as if hovering between sleeping and waking. As the characters walk forward into their future, Hardy advances into his past, seeking, in his ghostly phrase, 'the illusion of truth', knowing that the memory is of the inner world.

There is a difficulty, Hardy felt, in aligning the inner and the outer life, and this is related in his novels to the tug between the past and the present. Knowledge is change. The destruction of the old world by the new is the explicit subject of most of his novels. Hardy believes in the new. He feels the inevitability of change, of the destruction of the old, but the old is charged with more feeling than the new and he is always aware of the past in the present – his feeling is divided.

Thomas Hardy was an unusually creative man. His existence was one long process of making things, of turning feeling into form. He engaged in almost all the arts. He drew and painted in water colour. He was an architect. As a boy he played the fiddle well enough to be much in demand at country parties. He sang, set several texts to music and composed one or two pieces. He published fourteen novels, four collections of short stories and nine volumes of poetry as well as some scattered essays and occasional pieces. His first book of poetry appeared when he was fifty-eight. He wrote a tragedy and adapted some of his fiction for the stage. Hardy is remarkable for the diversity of his artistic accomplishments and is perhaps the only writer to be both a great novelist and a great poet.[10]

Fifty years after Hardy's death it is clear that he is one of the greatest English novelists, with Jane Austen and George Eliot, Henry James and Joseph Conrad. The capacity for feeling deeply depends on our capacity to mourn our losses and our guilt, and to bear this sadness. Hardy gives a shape to our feelings. Our sorrow is somehow transformed by his. He thought that all great things were done by men 'who were not at ease' and believed that his strength lay 'in a power of keeping going in most disheartening circumstances'.

NOTES

I would like to thank Caroline Rehder for all that she has contributed to my work and to express my appreciation to the students and colleagues with whom I have discussed Hardy, especially Michael Alexander, L. St. J. Butler, Felicity Riddy, Angela Smith and Grahame Smith. I would like to dedicate this essay to the memory of my mother, Marguerite McConkie Rehder.

My source for the information about Hardy's life and for his opinions, notes and letters, except where other references are given below, is his autobiography, Florence Hardy, *The Life of Thomas Hardy 1840–1928* (London, 1970, originally published in two volumes in 1928 and 1930 respectively). For Hardy's authorship of this work, see Richard L. Purdy, *Thomas Hardy, A Bibliographical Study* (Oxford, 1968) pp. 265–7, 272–3.

1   Virginia Woolf, *A Writer's Diary* (New York. 1954) pp. 88–93. There are a number of similar accounts. This is Arthur Compton Rickett's description of his first meeting with Hardy, in the summer of 1909: 'I had expected a bigger man, a man of the scholar type, one whose expression reflected the austere melancholy of his portrait. And here was a little man who looked like a country solicitor, with keen twinkling eyes and a quietly cordial manner. For a moment a look of fear flashed out. "You don't want to talk about my books?" Of course, I did, but mendaciously I assured him that I didn't. For I quickly divined that the interview would be short and unsatisfactory if I allowed my curiosity full play.' *I Look Back, Memories of Fifty Years* (London, 1933) pp. 176–7.

2   Wordsworth in his story about a murderer, *Guilt and Sorrow*, uses Stonehenge for a somewhat similar purpose.

3   Wallace Stevens, *Opus Posthumous* (New York, 1957) p. 255. The passage is from his preface to William Carlos Williams's *Collected Poems 1921–1931*.

4   See Erich Auerbach's brilliant account of how Christianity transformed the classical division of styles in his *Dante: Poet of the Secular World* (Chicago, 1961, originally published in 1929) pp. 1–23, and *Literary Language and Its Public in Late Latin Antiquity and in the Middle Ages* (London, 1965) pp. 27–66. Hardy is very much an inheritor and an innovator in this transformed tradition.

5   Gordon S. Haight, *George Eliot* (Oxford, 1969) p. 195.

6   I owe the basis of this sentence to Professor S. S. Prawer of Oxford who, in a very interesting paper on 'Karl Marx and World Literature' read to the conference on Problems and Methodology of Comparative Literature (Norwich, 17 December 1975), called Marx 'an Eminent Victorian' and said that his 'critical temperament resembled that of Matthew Arnold'.

7   Thomas Hardy, *Desperate Remedies* (London, 1953) p. 13.

8   Thomas Hardy, *An Indiscretion in the Life of an Heiress*, edited with an

Introduction by Terry Coleman (London, 1976) p. 17; Robert Gittings, *Young Thomas Hardy* (London, 1975) pp. 102–3.

9 Thomas Hardy, 'The Science of Fiction', *New Review* (April 1891), reprinted in *Thomas Hardy's Personal Writings*, edited by H. Orel (London, 1967) p. 135.

10 The other authors who come to mind are Goethe, Scott, Hugo and Lawrence.

3 Hardy and the Hag

John Fowles

> — Then meseemed it the guise of the ranker Venus,
> Named of some Astarte, of some Cotytto.
> Down I knelt before it and kissed the panel,
> Drunk with the lure of love's inhibited dreamings.
>
> Till the dawn I rubbed, when there gazed up at me
> A hag, that had slowly emerged from under my hands there,
> Pointing the slanted finger towards a bosom
> Eaten away of a rot from the lusts of a lifetime . . .
> — I could have ended myself in heart-shook horror.
>   'The Collector Cleans His Picture'

> 'I am under a doom, Somers. Yes, I am under a doom.'
>   *The Well-Beloved*

*   *   *

Most English novelists, however happy to indulge in literary gossip, are fanatically shy of talking of the realities of their private imaginative lives, just as they entertain an ancient preference for a narrating persona that is above all unpretentious and clubbable – a predilection that extends well beyond the strict arctic (where all is Snow) of the middle-class novel. I believe this proceeds far more from the cunning puritan in our make-up (our fear that investigation of the unconscious may lessen the pleasure we derive from being its playground) than from some fatuous association between amateurishness and gentlemanliness. The simple truth is that novel-writing is an onanistic and taboo-laden pursuit, and therefore socially shameful to the more conforming and morally dubious to the more fastidious. Hemingway's is only an extreme case of the kind of public mask knowledge of this truth forces most novelists to assume.

Yet we English have been so successful at the novel – and at poetry – very much because of this tension between private reality and public pretence. If the glory of the French is to be naked and lucid about what they really feel, and make, ours is to be veiled and oblique. I do not see this as evidence of our finer taste and greater seemliness. I think we just enjoy it more that way, in bed as in books; for the second simple truth is that creating another world, however imperfectly, is a haunting, isolating and guilt-ridden experience, very similar indeed to the creating of a 'real' perspective on the actual world that every child must undertake. As with the child, this experience is heavy with loss – of all the discarded illusions and counter-myths as well as of the desires and sensibilities that inexorable adulthood (or artistic good form) has no time for.

The cost of it is a constant grumbling ground-bass in the Hardy novel I wish to consider, *The Well-Beloved*. Pierston-Hardy feels cursed by his 'inability to ossify', to mature like other men. He feels himself arrested in eternal youth; yet also knows (the empty maturity of his contemporaries, such as Somers, gets savagely short shrift elsewhere) that the artist who does not keep a profound part of himself not just open to his past, but *of* his past, is like an electrical system without a current. When Pierston finally elects to be 'mature', he is dead as an artist.

A seriously attempted novel is also deeply exhausting of the writer's psyche, since the new world created must be torn from the world in his head. In a highly territorial species like man, such repeated loss of secret self must in the end have a quasi-traumatic effect. This may be why – like many novelists – I cannot think very critically of Hardy; there is too strong a sense of shared trap, a shared predicament. In any case I have long felt that the academic world spends far too much time on the written text and far too little on the benign psychosis of the writing experience; on particular product rather than general process. Equivalents of the now dominant ethological approach (the living behaviour) in zoology are sadly lacking in the world of letters. This is what I should like to try here with the Hardy of *The Well-Beloved*, not least because with this approach the artistically less excellent may often be the 'behaviourally' more revealing. If space had allowed I should have liked also to examine his two earliest fictions, *An Indiscretion in the Life of an Heiress* and *Desperate Remedies*. They already unconsciously bare much that was to be deliberately exposed in his last novel.

I should add that my main private interest in life has always been nature, not literature – understanding function rather than making value-judgements; and secondly, that if I may seem to cite personal experience too frequently, my aim is emphatically not to suggest invidious comparisons, but to try to explain a little the view from the inside: some of the natural, and unnatural, history of my peculiar sub-species.

*   *   *

By supposing the ubiquitous scamping of technique and the almost algebraic impatience with anything but the basic formulae of his fiction to have been intentional on Hardy's part, I have over the years tried to see *The Well-Beloved* as a black farce. But even if that were the original premise (as the very last lines of the 1892 version hint), its execution was badly botched. Taken straight, the book cannot be judged as anything but a disastrous failure by Hardy's standards elsewhere. Indeed I think its closest cousin in modern English writing is that last spew of bile from H. G. Wells, *Mind at the End of its Tether* – which, the reader may recall, despatched rather more than mind to eternal oblivion. ('The end of everything we call life is close at hand and cannot be evaded.') Despite the avuncular preface from 1912, *The Well-Beloved*, seething as it is with the suppressed rage of the self-duped, is fiction at the end of its tether. It is also the closest conducted tour we shall ever have of the psychic process behind Hardy's written product. No biography will ever take us so deep.

One thinks of Hoffmann, of the maker whose automata become so lifelike that they enslave him. But here it is a stage worse: the case of a god whose supposedly living Adams and Eves are now seen to be a tatter of *trompe-l'oeil*, a creak of cogs and levers – and who can only abscond in horror from the realisation that he himself is the arch-automaton. There is evidence that this grim revelation, accompanied by Hardy's equally grim disillusion with his marriage, was dawning long before the 1892 version of the story. However, two failures in his own self-destructive logic in that version (to be mentioned later) suggest that he had not yet fully seen his 'sickness'. There is also the striking enigma that the two versions of this technically worst novel span the writing of one of the finest, *Jude the Obscure*. That, too, I hope to explain in part.

Hardy's nightmare is painfully familiar to most contemporary novelists. The question of whether fiction is at the end of its tether is now universally in the air. It comes to us, far more consciously, as a nausea at the fictionality of fiction (less of a tautology than it may seem), or as a dread of once more entering an always ultimately defeating labyrinth. No further explanation is needed of the marked drop in fertility that has beset novelists during the last fifty years. The more you are aware of a hopeless obsession, the less you are driven by it. This is why *The Well-Beloved* is infinitely the most important of all Hardy's books for a practising or intending writer of fiction to establish an attitude towards. The others, his far greater novels in ordinary terms, are now Victorian monuments, safe prey for the literary surveyors. *The Well-Beloved* still waits, potent, like a coiled adder on the Portland cliffs that brood distantly on where I sit, across Lyme Bay.

* * *

I had the interesting experience, a few years ago, of being psycho-analysed by proxy – through one of my novels, *The French Lieu-tenant's Woman*. Professor Gilbert J. Rose, who teaches clinical psychiatry at Yale, wrote a good paper on the book, but I was rather more interested in his general theory of what produces the artistically creative mind, since it largely confirmed – and greatly clarified – intuitive conclusions of my own.

In simple terms his proposition was that some children retain a particularly rich memory of the passage from extreme infancy, when the identity of the baby is merged with that of the mother, to the arrival of the first awareness of separate identity and the simul-taneous first dawn of what will become the adult sense of reality; that is, they are deeply marked by the passage from a unified magical world to a discrete 'realist' one. What seemingly stamps itself in-delibly on this kind of infant psyche is a pleasure in the fluid, polymorphic nature of the sensuous impressions, visual, tactile, auditory and the rest, that he receives; and so profoundly that he cannot, even when the detail of this intensely auto-erotic experience has retreated into the unconscious, refrain from tampering with reality – from trying to recover, in other words, the early oneness with the mother that granted this ability to make the world mysteriously and deliciously change meaning and appearance. He was once a magician with a wand; and given the right other predisposing and environmental factors, he will one day devote his life to trying to regain the unity and the power by recreating adult versions of the experience . . . he will be an artist. Moreover, since every child goes through some variation of the same experience, this also ex-plains one major attraction of art for the audience. The artist is simply someone who does the journey back for the less conditioned and less technically endowed.[1]

I do not know on how much empirical evidence Professor Rose's theory is based, but I find it a plausible and valuable model. One enigma about all artists, however successful they may be in worldly or critical terms, is the markedly repetitive nature of their endeavour – the inability not to return again and again on the same impossible journey. One must posit here an unconscious drive towards an unattainable. The theory also accounts for the sense of irrecoverable loss (or predestined defeat) so characteristic of many major novelists, and not least of Thomas Hardy in particular.[2] Associated with this is a permanent – and symptomatically childlike – dissatisfaction with reality as it is, the 'adult' world that is the case. Here too one must posit a deep memory of ready entry into alternative worlds – a dominant nostalgia for what Hardy called metempsychosis.

Beyond the specific myth of each novel, the novelist longs to be possessed by the continuous underlying myth he entertains of himself – a state not to be attained by method, logic, self-analysis, intelligent judgement or any other of the qualities that make a good teacher, executive or scientist. I should find it very hard to define what constitutes this being possessed, yet I know when I am and when I am not; that there are markedly different degrees of the state; that it functions as much by exclusion as by awareness; and above all, that it remains childlike in its fertility of lateral inconsequence, its setting of adultly ordered ideas in flux. Indeed, the workbench cost of this possession is revision – the elimination of the childish from the childlike, both in the language and the conception. Like Venus and Cupid, each muse has her accompanying imp. It is also a state that withdraws (like the Well-Beloved) as the text nears consummation; and its disappearance, however pleased one is with the final cast, is always deeply distressing . . . one other sense of loss, or reluctant return to normality, that every novelist-child has to contend with.

This obsessive need to find Pierston's 'conduit into space' – to transcend present reality – opens a Pandora's box of associated problems in more ordinary life. One I wish to discuss, partly because it is so generally ignored, partly because I believe it very important with Hardy, is that of marital guilt. No one who spends most of his life in pursuit of a chimera can live comfortably with his everyday self or that of the person closest to him. At one level he must know that for as long as he is on his voyage the central emotional truth of his life is not where it should be; at another, that he is constantly, if only imaginatively, betraying his wife in other ports. It is easy to dismiss the first Mrs Hardy; but I have no doubt that she underwent many years of feeling herself shuffled off – in some cases, flagrantly travestied – by the man she married. I am equally sure that, 'drunk with the lure of love's inhibited dreamings', her husband knew it.

One may view the wife's predicament in terms of an important sub-theme of *The Well-Beloved*: the conflict between the Pagan and the Christian on Portland – Portland as the combined arena, peninsula-womb and *domaine perdu* of Hardy's imagination. If the Pagan there stands for permitted incest, pre-marital relations, the unchecked Id, it also stands for consummation; and if the Christian stands for current social convention (as in the first Avice's 'modern feelings' about staying chaste), the Super-Ego and 'mainland' reality in general, it also forbids consummation . . . in other words, it forbids what

Hardy as a writer needs to have forbidden. The role of a wife in this conflict (and some such polarised tension between creative 'desire' and social 'duty' will exist in every novelist's mind) is complex. The one trait of the permissive Pagan she possesses, available presence, is the one the writer does not need; and in all else she stands against the cherished dream – she is the Marcia without make-up of the final chapter of *The Well-Beloved*, the 'real' reality, armed with the sanctity of the conventional institution, and so on. Her function and value is therefore certain to be oxymoronic to her husband's creative self : if she is potentially the strongest ally of his conscious, outward self, she can equally seem the greatest threat to his inward, unconscious one.

There is a further complicating factor. An essential part of the novelist's mental equipment is an iconogenic faculty, which is crystalloid (repetitive of structure) in process – and certainly, like the crystal, needs a stable nurturing culture. Though the wife is the mortal enemy of the mother as Ashtaroth-Aphrodite, she is also required to assume a rather more practical aspect of maternity – protective Jocasta against the cruel Laius of the review columns.

This relationship is in my experience a far more important consideration in the writing and shaping of a novel than most critics and biographers seem prepared to allow. We must also remember that the voyage undertaken is back to an indulged primal self and all its pleasures, and that the main source of those pleasures was that eternal other woman, the mother. The vanished young mother of infancy is quite as elusive as the Well-Beloved – indeed, she *is* the Well-Beloved, although the adult writer transmogrifies her according to the pleasures and fancies that have in the older man superseded the nameless ones of the child – most commonly into a young female sexual ideal of some kind, to be attained or pursued (or denied) by himself hiding behind some male character. In one extraordinary and very revealing early case Hardy hid behind a female stalking-horse – Miss Aldclyffe in *Desperate Remedies*. The transmogrification can also, of course, be vindictive, as in so much of *The Well-Beloved*, or in any novel where woman is treated as the betrayer of Adam. Both transmogrifications, into the idolised love-object or the unforgiven 'whore', may very often be seen side-by-side in the same novel.

Against this constant emotional fugue must be set the real presence of the woman the novelist shares his life with. She is bound willy-nilly to take on the face of the moral (in Hardy's case, the 'Christian') censor; and this can seriously alter both the shape of a text and the general tenor of the novelist's career. I am convinced this was the case with Hardy, who had the additional problem of a childless marriage to contend with. There is his lifelong need, self-parodied in *The Well-Beloved*, to avoid consummation. I cannot believe his reasons were solely artistic, or some effect of 'natural reticence'. A much closer reality had to be placated.

For me this plays an important part in explaining the extraordinary difference in the quality of his last two novels. I can see the two attempts at *The Well-Beloved* only as an admission of sin;[3] and *Jude the Obscure* as a 'recklessly pleasant'[4] relapse into the enduring obsession – almost a case of a burglar so relishing his penitential memoirs that he is driven back to the old game. I do not know how Mrs Hardy could not have seen more of herself in Arabella than in Sue Bridehead; or, even in the intended *mea culpa* itself – since the obsession remained far stronger than the will to repent – more of herself in Marcia and Nicola Pine-Avon (both 'corpses' as soon as they become amenable) than in the three Avices, even if she did not know they stood for the three Sparks sisters. In short, *The Well-Beloved* was less for a public audience than to assuage a private guilt. This also explains a great deal of its cursory impatience with realism, and the obfuscating classification under 'Romances and Fantasies'. Essentially the damage was long done, and the would-be 'Christian' husband must have known his cause was hopeless. The only proof of real contrition lay in silence; and even the genuineness of that proof is suspect, since self-exposure to his public in such matters must become more and more painful to a writer far from regardless of his conventional reputation and social status.

I hasten to add that I am not suggesting Hardy would have been a finer writer if he had been less trammelled, more frank. In practical terms this form of marital censorship is far more generally a valuable check on excess – the real woman in one's life symbolising both social consensus and artistic common sense – than an unhappy stifling. But what must often remain, alas, is a reciprocal accusation: on the wife's side – with far more justice – of imaginative infidelity and *mauvaise foi*, of being unfairly condemned as inadequate in a situation where the desired adequacy (erotic elusiveness, unattainability) is plainly impossible; and on the husband's side – much less reasonably – of lack of pity (plentifully demonstrated in Pierston for himself) over his 'disease'. Fair-copying wives know far better than anyone else the extent to which texts are lived in the writer's mind; and a final aggravating factor is the very specific and detailed way in which the novelist, given the length and dominance of realism in the form, is obliged to body forth his infidelity – 'the carnate dwelling-place of the haunting minion of his imagination', in a stiffly embarrassed phrasing from *The Well-Beloved* itself. I suspect one strong reason Hardy reserved himself to poetry after 1896 is precisely because verse is, in this context, a less 'naked' medium than prose; not an exposed field, but a shady copse.

*   *   *

Since it is in the nature of pleasure to wish to prolong itself, the writer will always invent obstacles (such as Hardy's favourite hurdles, malign coincidence and class difference) to his hunt of the Well-Beloved – one further cruel-vital function for the wife, it may be noted. But because the real goal is eternally doomed to failure, its attainment no more feasible than that the words on the page can become the scene they describe, the fundamental nature of the hunt is tragic. The happy ending, the symbolic marriage between hero-author and heroine-mother, is in this light mere wish-fulfilment, childish longing of the kind reflected in the traditional last sentence of all fairy stories. This is another major psychological dilemma (in his myth of himself) for the novelist, and one in which Hardy, by so often choosing the unhappy solution, foreshadowed our own century.

However, his choosing the 'reality' against the 'dream' cannot be explained simply in terms of a pessimistic temperament and a deterministic philosophy – of a put-upon Atreid cursing the unkind gods. To a psyche like Hardy's, both highly devious and highly erotic, it is not at all axiomatic that the happy consummation is more pleasurable. The cathartic effect of tragedy bears a resemblance to the unresolved note on which some folk-music ends; whereas there is something in the happy ending that resolves not only the story, but the need to embark on further stories. If the writer's secret and deepest joy is to search for an irrecoverable experience, the ending that announces that the attempt has once again failed may well seem more satisfying. Like the phoenix, Tess in ashes is Tess, under another name, released and reborn. In the deeper continuum of an artist's life, where the doomed and illicit hunt is still far more attractive than no hunt at all, the 'sad' may therefore be much happier than the 'happy' ending. It will be both releasing and therapeutic.

If this seems paradoxical, I can call only on personal experience. I wrote and printed two endings to *The French Lieutenant's Woman* entirely because from early in the first draft I was torn intolerably between wishing to reward the male protagonist (my surrogate) with the woman he loved and wishing to deprive him of her – that is, I wanted to pander to both the adult and the child in myself. I had experienced a very similar predicament in my two previous novels. Yet I am now very clear that I am happier, where I gave two, with the unhappy ending, and not in any way for objective critical reasons, but simply because it has seemed more fertile and onward to my whole being as a writer.

From the very beginning, from the schoolroom of *An Indiscretion*, there can be seen in Hardy a violent distaste for resolution, or consummation. The chance of happiness is almost always put in jeopardy by physical contact, the first hint of possession. His two earliest heroines, Geraldine and Cytherea, both behave absurdly like startled roe deer when they are first kissed; and their continuing capacity for not fulfilling their respective lovers', and the reader's, expectations exhibits a striking lack of psychological realism in a young writer who already showed ample command of it with less emotive characters. Even then it is clear Hardy finds his deepest pleasure in the period when consummation remains a distant threat, a bridge whose crossing – or collapse – can be put off for another chapter.

I think it must be said that this endlessly repeated luring-denying nature of his heroines is not too far removed from what our more vulgar age calls the cock-tease. It is a very characteristic movement – advancing, retreating, unveiling, re-veiling – of the meetings in *The Well-Beloved* and, as with so much else, done with the angry disregard of a man forced to lampoon himself. The actual sexual consummations in both versions are totally without erotic quality, indeed merely recorded by implication; and bring nothing but disillusion to both partners.

This leads me to that most Hardyesque of all narrative devices: the tryst. The isolated meeting of a man and woman, preferably by chance, preferably in 'pagan' nature and away from the 'Christian' restraint of town and house, preferably trap-set with various minor circumstances – whose introduction often shows Hardy at his weakest, as if emotional pressure choked invention – that oblige a greater closeness and eventual bodily contact . . . all this was transparently a more exciting concept than the 'all-embracing indifference'[5] of marriage.

Significantly Hardy always gives the trysting Well-Beloved the same physiological reaction – the rush of blood to the cheeks. This tumescent sexual metaphor is once again used to the point of self-satire in the present novel – Marcia is 'inflamed to peony hues', and so on. One may see a disguised death-wish where the first bodily contact is so perversely made the secret trigger (not *post*, but *ante coitum tristitia*) of the frustration and misery to come. But I suspect this predilection for the first faint erection of love, and the distaste for the thereafter of it, is one of Hardy's more enduring attractions. He had his finger on a very common death-wish, if such it is.

The importance of the tryst becomes clear when we realise that the Well-Beloved is never a face, but the congeries of affective circumstances in which it is met; as soon as it inhabits one face, its erotic energy (that is, the author's imaginative energy) begins to drain away. Since it cannot be the face of the only true, and original, Well-Beloved, it becomes a lie, is marked for death. In other words, the tryst is not the embodiment of a transient hope in the outward narrative so much as a straight desire for transience, since gaining briefly to lose eternally is the chief fuel of the imagination in Hardy himself. In *The Well-Beloved* this is shown in the highly voyeuristic treatment of the early relationship with the second Avice; and in the corollary masochistic – or 'Christian' – misery of their life in Pierston's London flat . . . where the girl is put, with a ghastly irony, to 'dust all my Venus failures'.

Plainly the tryst is also a scarcely concealed simulacrum of the primary relationship of the child with the vanished mother. In *The Well-Beloved*, when Marcia and Pierston retreat from the storm under the tarred and upturned lerret, foetally crouched since they cannot stand, the model is particularly clear. He could 'feel her furs against him'; he thinks of himself as playing Romeo to her Juliet, implicitly breaking a taboo far greater than that dividing two rival families. As they walk on to Weymouth he goes on thinking 'how soft and warm the lady was in her fur covering, as he held her so tightly; the only dry spots in the clothing of either being her left side and his right, where they excluded the rain by their mutual pressure'; and then finally there is the strange near-fetichist scene, the most overtly erotic in the book, when Pierston dries Marcia's wet clothes at the inn . . . manipulates the veils, while the baggageless dancer stands naked in his imagination, if not his sight, upstairs.

Nor can it be a coincidence that incest plays so large a part in the novel, not only in its triple-goddess central theme, but also in the Portland setting. There are constant references to shared blood relationships; the second and third Avices live in Pierston's natal house, even in his former room there; the kimberlin, or non-Portlander, is unmistakably associated with the Oedipal father, the frustrator of the dream, the intruder in the primal unity. In the 1892 version Hardy followed the lerret scene with the marriage of Pierston and Marcia, instead of the more casual hotel liaison of the final revision. He also had Pierston marry the third Avice in the earlier text. These were both, it seems to me, errors of his unconscious, results of a lingering desire to give himself, behind his hero, some reward – characteristically enough, in the form of a sanction on the Pagan by a 'Christian' institution. But on reflection he must have seen that this was the last novel – last novel indeed – in which he could indulge such conditioned wish-fulfilment.[6] When all is to reveal the tyranny, it is absurd to behave at its behest. One cannot exorcise witches – least of all the ultimate witch – by symbolically marrying them.

This *abnormally* close juxtaposition, or isolating, of a male and a female character is so constant a feature of the male novel that I think it adds further support to Professor Rose's theory. I know myself how excitement mounts – if there had been a Creator, how much he must have looked forward to the chapter of Eden – as such situations approach and how considerably their contrivance can alter preceding narrative. Though I gained the outward theme of *The Collector* from a bizarre real-life incident in the 1950s, similar fantasies had haunted my adolescence – not, let me quickly say, with the cruelties and criminalities of the book, but very much more along the lines of the Hardy tryst. That is, I dreamed isolating situations with girls reality did not permit me isolation with: the desert island, the aircrash with two survivors, the stopped lift, the rescue from a fate worse than death . . . all the desperate remedies of the romantic novelette; but also, more valuably, countless variations of the chance meeting in more realistic contexts. A common feature of such fantasies was some kind of close confinement, like Hardy's lerret, where the Well-Beloved was obliged to notice me; and I realise, in retrospect, that my own book was a working-out of the futility, in reality, of expecting well of such metaphors for the irrecoverable relationship. I had the very greatest difficulty in killing off my own heroine; and I have only quite recently, in a manner I trust readers will now guess, understood the real meaning of my ending . . . the way in which the monstrous and pitiable Clegg (the man who acts out his own fantasies) prepares for a new 'guest' in the Bluebeard's cell beneath his lonely house. It is a very grave fallacy that novelists understand the personal application of their own novels. I suspect in fact that it is generally the last face of them that they decipher. Just as the Well-Beloved passes from glimpsed woman to woman in our private lives, so does it in our characters. This is one other principal reason why we can, as we grow older, kill them off with so little real pain. Creating an embodiment of the Well-Beloved is like marrying her; and she would never stand for that.

In his recent biography I was taken to task by Dr Robert Gittings for having swallowed whole the Tryphena 'myth'. Though I would, accepting both the biographical and the autobiographical evidence in *The Well-Beloved* itself, concede at once that the likelihood of there having been only one Tryphena in Hardy's life is non-existent, I remain a total apostate when it comes to dismissing this type of experience as unimportant. The reference to Tryphena's death (in 1890) in the preface to *Jude the Obscure* cannot be ignored; nor can I think what else, or who else, could have delayed the smashing of the psychic generator, apparently already decided on by 1889, to enable that last great output of fictional power. There is reinforcing evidence of her potency in the present book, in the scene (Part Two,

Chapter 3) where the London high society in which Pierston finds himself fades to nothingness before 'the lily-white corpse of an obscure country-girl'; he refers to the 'almost radiant purity of this new-sprung affection for a flown spirit'. The very title of the chapter – stylistically one of the best written and emotionally one of the most deeply felt in the book – is 'She becomes an inaccessible ghost'.

If the Well-Beloved ever took a quasi-perennial 'carnate' form in Hardy's life, I believe it was in the 'charm idealized by lack of substance' of the Tryphena of the Weymouth summer of 1869.[7] The outward of the Well-Beloved may flit from shape to shape; but she is also a spirit, and spirit inheres much more tenaciously in its most powerful original manifestation. Pierston says of the second Avice that 'He could not help seeing in her all that he knew of another, and veiling in her all that did not harmonize with his sense of metempsychosis.' And when the second Avice later plays tacit procuress, at Pierston's command, to her own daughter, we are surely to see that the Well-Beloved, if discontinuous in the epiphany, is one in the genesis. After all, it is not only novelists who cherish and recall first loves most dearly and deeply.

We know the very practical and vital role played in Hardy's creative life by his mother, Jemima Hand; of his long tryst with her at Bockhampton during the writing of his first indisputable master-piece, *Far from the Madding Crowd*. We know, in Dr Gittings' words, 'He was attracted again and again by the same type of woman, a replica of his own mother, with the striking features shared by all women of the Hand family' – of which one was the eyebrows like musical slurs reflected in the 'glide upon glide' Hardy used to describe the heroine of the novel he was writing during the 1869 summer. We know of his previous attraction to Tryphena's sister, Martha; how closely a dry shrewdness in each of the Avices echoes a similar quality in the three sisters of real life and in Jemima herself; how exactly the social differences between the second and third Avices parallel the 'peasant' and 'educated' sides of Tryphena. We also know how resolutely Hardy ostracised his 'pagan' relations after the mid-1870s – thus making his continuing use of them in his fiction and imagination doubly illicit. Hardy may have seen the emotional tug-of-war between Emma Gifford and Tryphena in the early 1870s only in terms of pain and suffering; but it seems clear that this is where the Well-Beloved first *consciously* manifested herself in his life, never to leave it again. Marriage simply meant that her lasting dominance was assured, and that his wife from then on was con-demned to the punishment foreshadowed in the poem 'Near Lanivet, 1872' – 'In the running of Time's far glass,/Her crucified . . .'

Of course it would be absurd to suppose that Hardy ever realised who truly lay behind Tryphena and all the other incarnations of the Well-Beloved, and indeed I suspect the power – and frequency – of a novelist's output is very much bound up with his failing to realise it; and that we later novelists have yet to come to terms with the knowledge. If ignorance here can hardly be termed bliss, it is certainly more fertile.[8] The difficult reality is that, if in every human and daily way ('In one I can atone for all') the actual woman in a novelist's life is of indispensable importance to him, imaginatively it is the lost ones who count, firstly because they stand so perfectly for the original lost woman and secondly (but perhaps no less importantly) because they are a prime source of fantasy and of guidance, like Ariadne with her thread, in the labyrinth of his other worlds.

Because they were never truly possessed, they remain eternally malleable and acquiescent, like the sculptor's lay model. The repeated use to which they can be put may even finally suggest a fuller possession of them than any mere real or carnal knowledge could ever have allowed. And this above all is why, to the extent that a creator of fiction needs such a figure behind his principal heroines, he is unlikely to want to grant her even imaginary happiness at the end of the narrative; and must therefore deny it to himself in the male character who is his surrogate. Hardy seems to have grasped this indispensable corollary under the shock of the suicide of Horace Moule, since it is first clearly enunciated in the fate allotted Farmer Boldwood. From then on the doomed and thwarted child sits firm inside all his major male characters. They too become phoenixes; sacrificed, so that their sacrificer may once again summon up the Well-Beloved and her further victim. Lost, denying and denied, she lives and remains his; given away, consummated, she dies.

This is the redeeming secret behind all the self-disgust in *The Well-Beloved*. If superficially the three Avices may be seen (by the reader) as sadistic sirens, luring the poor sailor to his death in the Race, or (by Pierston-Hardy) as the trumpery puppets of his own morbid and narcissistic imagination, more deeply I view them as something quite contrary: the maternal muses who grant the power to comprehend and palliate the universal condition of mankind, which is, given the ability of the human mind to choose and imagine other than the chosen or the actual course of events, a permanent state of loss. I spoke earlier of the book lying like a coiled adder on the cliffs of the Isle of Slingers, but I think finally that it contains its own antidote. It remains a grave warning; but against the sailor, not the voyage.

And then surely, in the last account, one has to smile. Who, faced with the hell of being a true and deeply loved artist ('how incomparably the immaterial dream dwarfed the grandest of substantial things') and the paradise of being Mr Alfred Somers, that 'middle-aged family man with spectacles', painting for 'the furnishing householder through the middling critic', would not still rush to tryst with the hag, and book a seat on the first broomstick down to Bockhampton?

NOTES

1 Sensitive female readers may not be too happy about the pronoun of this paragraph, but the theory helps explain why all through more recent human history men seem better adapted – or more driven – to individual artistic expression than women. Professor Rose points out that the chance of being conditioned by this primal erotic experience is (if one accepts Freudian theory) massively loaded towards the son. The novel is, of course, something of an exception to the general rule, but even there the characteristic male preoccupation with loss, non-fulfilment, non-consummation, is usually lacking in women writers. I can think of only two, among the great, who seem clearly to have been 'fixed' in the normal male way: Emily Brontë and Virginia Woolf. Perhaps the masculine component in their psyches was stronger.

2 Although this sense of loss does not give automatic birth to the tragic novelist. It may generate irony and comedy in the writer, and indeed has preponderantly done so in the English novel, perhaps because the comic is, given our national penchant for the veiled and oblique, a better public mask over the basic situation. Waugh and Nabokov exhibit interesting alternations of reaction – 'tragic-naked' and 'comic-concealed' – in this context. Hardy evidently attempted the latter in *The Well-Beloved*. But the true comic novelist dulls the loss by mocking it.

3 Not least because the self-flagellation is so overdone. When Pierston terms the experience of the Well-Beloved as 'anything but pleasure', 'a racking spectacle', 'a ghost story', I must reach for the salt-cellar. It is also noticeable that the flagellant's loudest (and least convincing) cries are usually given a 'Christian' colouring. 'I have lost a faculty, for which loss Heaven be praised!'

4 Pierston feels the Well-Beloved shift from Nicola to the second Avice. 'A gigantic satire upon the mutations of his nymph during the last twenty years seemed looming . . . But it was recklessly pleasant to leave the suspicion unrecognized as yet, and follow the lead.'

5 The phrase is used of the second Avice's marriage to Ike: '. . . having as its chief ingredient neither love nor hate, but an all-embracing indifference'.

6 Although there is an interesting relic of what one might call the sultan syndrome in male novelists in the final paragraph of Chapter 8 in Part Two. Pierston thinks of 'packing' the second Avice off to school – finishing her in all senses! – and then marrying her and 'taking his chance'.

7 Lack of substance was already inherent in the affaire, long before the final separator, Emma Gifford, appeared in March 1870. Tryphena's hopes of going to Stockwell Normal College, and the strict propriety of conduct expected of candidates, must have borne a 'Christian' connotation to Hardy. Already loss offered itself, and the frustation of the pagan-permissive.

8 Thus in my view the characteristic abundance of the Victorian novel –
   and novelist – can partly be attributed to the taboo on sexual frankness,
   which in turn prevented the potentially inhibiting awareness of underlying
   psychic process. In short, outward sexual 'honesty' in the novel may be
   creatively far more limiting (or lethal, if *The Well-Beloved* is to be believed)
   than we generally imagine.

4 The Improving Hand. The New Wessex edition of the *Complete Poems*

Robert Gittings

Hardy as a poet is still an area where people can differ, dispute, form quite individual likes and dislikes, find – a familiar miracle, this – superb poems, which, they would swear, have eluded for years their devoted reading. Above all, and perhaps blessedly, as a poet he too eludes much academic and pontifical generalisation. We all know by now what a gaffe T. S. Eliot made when he tried to patronise and damn with faint – very faint – praise Hardy's achievements as a poet. Only Eliot's countryman, Henry James, has outdone Eliot's snobbish dismissal of Hardy's work as the self-expression of a self hardly worth expressing. One is at once reminded of James writing to Stevenson about *Tess*: 'Oh, yes, dear Louis . . . The pretence of sexuality is only equalled by the absence of it.' If the test of a great poet is to make high-falutin' critics angry, then 'the good little Thomas Hardy' (James's phrase again) passes in the first class of poets. Gloomily anticipating such critics when he brought out his first book of verses, Hardy wrote to Gosse: 'I do not expect a particularly gracious reception of them', while faced with his own first American critic, Professor W. L. Phelps, a few years later, Hardy was 'evidently pained' at the latter's somewhat casual dismissal of his poems, and took his revenge, it seems, by giving Phelps not the literary discussion he hoped, but an extensive lecture on the cats frequenting Max Gate.

And now, at last and not before it was due, the poems *can* all be read, literally and physically. Formerly, whenever one found that some intelligent person did not really know Hardy's poems, he would reply in extenuation, 'Well, I can't stand that collected edition, with all the poems so close together that your eye can't take in any one of them.' It is, I think, fair to say that the previous reprints of the collected poems put more people off Hardy the poet than they gained him admirers. It was exactly like 'that scrofulous French novel' in Browning's *Soliloquy of the Spanish Cloister* –

On grey paper with blunt type!

Well, now, belated amends have handsomely been made. The new *Complete Poems* is a large, clear, comfortably-spaced volume, a pleasure to the eye and a revelation to one's appreciation of Hardy's poetic stature. For the first time, the poems seem to come to meet you on the page. Clear type has also helped accuracy, and the commas and other points that had blurred or even disappeared are put back as Hardy intended by the conscientious and highly-informed editorial care of James Gibson. One only wishes he had been entrusted, while he was about it, with the variorum edition, whose absence is still one of the great blots on Hardy scholarship, and which Mr Gibson is surely, of all editors, the most fitted to provide.

And now that we can read them, what about the poems? The first consideration to a biographer like myself, though not, of course, by any means the most important thing about them, is their intense biographical significance now that they can be comprehended as a whole. Like nearly every innovatory poet, Hardy had to create his own mythology. One thinks of Wordsworth, rejecting the classical mythology of the Augustans, and impelled to create a pantheon of ideal references out of the natural objects that surrounded him in the Lakes, where rock, fell, tree and flower took the place of the old gods and goddesses. Similarly Hardy, rejecting an easy dependence on a vague sub-Wordsworthian pantheism – though his first known poem, as this volume shows, was totally Wordsworthian – sought for an entirely new set of myths to fit his own very concrete and minutely observant verse. He found it in a way which, so far as I know, is unique to himself. He projected the main events of his life as his own mythological system, and used them as universal terms of reference. To give an exactly practical example, after the death of his first wife in 1912, he tended to use in all poems – that is, astonishingly, half of his whole life's published output – a mythology based on events, times, and places in the personal story of his forty-two-and-a-half years' relationship with Emma. Without their story – and this is one of the rewarding features of Hardy biography – many poems are a set of meaningless and irritatingly mysterious symbols.

Take, for instance, the poem called 'A Procession of Dead Days', which may perhaps stand for an 'average' Hardy poem, not in the first flight nor low down on the list, and therefore a subject for fair analysis. It has eight stanzas, each representing a 'day' of a different character : the last two stanzas spread over one such day, so that there are in fact seven days described in all.The first starts at dawn and takes Hardy to a strange spot; the second is warmer, rosy and joyful; the third foggy, but bringing 'the kiss' and new maturity to the poet; the fourth has 'a rainbow shine of promise'; the fifth has 'morning clothes' of 'misty blue' and marks 'a meteor act'; the sixth brings 'an iron rod' of ominous aspect; the seventh and last is early in the morning, 'bringing that which numbs', and depriving the poet in the grey early light of 'the third hour'. The symbolism, baffling at first, is entirely clear when one realises the mythic structure. Each day is an actual event in the lives of Emma and Thomas Hardy. As in all his later poems, cold March is the time of their Cornish meeting, warm August the time of falling in love, foggy October, of love recognised, June (or some summer month), of love promised. Number five 'in his morning clothes' of 'misty blue' is both a reference to their church wedding (morning dress) and the mild, September Keatsian mists, when the ceremony occurred, the month symbolising happiness through Hardy's writing, as he reminds himself of that autumn day in 1874. The sixth, with its baleful 'rod', is probably some time in the 1890s, when, as in poems like 'The Dead Man Walking', Emma grew cold to him, while the gusty November morning of number seven is the hour in 1912 when Emma died. These symbols are repeated in all later poems; the falling leaves, blowing into his room in November, are symbols of death, August is always a rosy time of hope, even when raining. He has created a consistent, personal myth.

Other entirely personal symbols abound through this best one-half of his poetic output. 'My friend', always in the singular, is always based on Horace Moule, Hardy's boyhood mentor who took his own life in 1873. The poems 'An Experience', 'In the Seventies', 'Before my Friend Arrived', 'The Dead Man Walking' again and many others, use Moule's tragic death as a symbol both of living help and irretrievable loss. A whole clutch of poems uses the setting of a bleak and empty pond as a symbol of loss and parting, from 'Neutral Tones', written early in 1867, to 'At Rushy-Pond' and 'On a Heath' – no pond described, but herons, another loss symbol, show a pond is near – both of later date apparently. Of the types of women that emerge usually anonymously out of the verses Emma symbolises the adventurous past, flitting the Cornish cliffs, with hair 'nut-coloured' and 'rose-flush coming and going', while Florence Dugdale has (and indeed noticeably had) the 'large and luminous eye' of 'Had You Wept' and similar poems. Observance of these very exact symbols can correct criticism. A recent judgement that this latter poem is a fictional address by Clym Yeobright to Eustacia Vye would not have occurred if it had been realised that Florence's deep-set eyes always symbolise the sympathy and care for feelings that Hardy found in his association with her. Poems concerning 'the country girl', his sister Mary, use her as a symbol of the deepest ties of ancestral and blood relationship, another consistent theme in Hardy's verse, especially after her death in 1915.

In the sense that he uses these events private to his own life as universal symbols for poetry, Hardy is vulnerable to Eliot's gibe about expressing a self-centred attitude. The value to him was that it gave a set of referential terms on which he could base the deepest emotions, without fully giving his inner 'self' away too exactly. Poetry could be 'confessional', and yet have generalised meaning. This is what we feel about the most moving of Hardy's verses; never mind whether this or that girl or event or incident is being commemorated, the occasion has brought a response that forces itself painfully to our notice, without quite ever betraying its perhaps almost commonplace origins. We therefore find the most affecting and portentous meaning for us in poems of simple and often almost bald statement of what seem to be ordinary matters of fact.

In later revisions, Hardy often tends to blur the factual origins of such poems. It is therefore doubly valuable for us that Mr Gibson has been allowed, and has selected so admirably, nearly thirty pages of notes on the texts, though here again one can only wish he had been trusted with a full variorum treatment. These manuscripts and other variants show how Hardy scholarship for the past twenty years has been misled by R. L. Purdy's statement that 'all Hardy's poetical MSS [are] a fair copy with relatively few alterations.' Purdy, a superb bibliographer, is an arbitrary handler of textual matters, such as this, and has little idea of any inner biographical significance. For example, his lucid note on a poem passed off as Hardy's by an impostor, and entitled 'Two Roses', totally misses the point that there was a contemporary play with that exact title, whose association, for various reasons, would be calculated to embarrass Hardy. To get back to Purdy's original statement, it is, as anyone knows who has done any work on Hardy's poetic MSS, the precise opposite of the truth. Hardy was a born alterer, usually, but not always, for the better. These *are* fair copies, or rather they begin as such; but before sending them to the printer, Hardy has nearly everywhere made MS alterations of deep and sometimes far-reaching effect, at times changing the whole aspect of a poem. Purdy again claims to have noted 'the more important of these' but he has not. For the first time, Mr Gibson's wisely selected notes reveal these variants to us, and not infrequently change our whole conception of a poem, a stanza or a line. For example, in 'Wessex Heights', one of Hardy's most personal poems, and certainly one his most mysterious, interpretation has had a fine time with the 'ghost' who appears to Hardy

In the railway train whenever I do not want it near ...

Eager biographical speculators have seen this as the same picture as that of the small boy in the poem 'Midnight on the Great Western', and his verbal and emotional counterpart, the weird child arriving by train in *Jude the Obscure*. We have not, of course. been spared Hardy's suppostitious bastard boy. Yet the original MS, silently passed over by Purdy, was clearly

In the railway train whenever I do not want her there,

a change of sex which blows the mysterious boy away out of the carriage window, and shows that this part of the poem was, as Florence Hardy said, about some of the *women* Hardy knew. Gibson, incidentally, was not the first to point this out; but his choice to print this as the most significant variant in the poem shows the soundness of his editorial judgement.

Good editing, and biographical interest and insight apart, what does this new edition of the poems give us as ordinary readers of Hardy? The poems will certainly now be read, as I said, with more physical pleasure. The mental pleasure will not, I think, be much enhanced by the fresh batch of twenty-eight poems uncollected by Hardy himself. These, mostly already printed by authorities such as Evelyn Hardy and J. O. Bailey, do not add much to our admiration of Hardy the poet, and in one instance lessen our love for Hardy the man. A man in his late eighties may do strange things on his deathbed. Yet perhaps more macabre than any story Hardy ever wrote is the incident in his last days when he insisted on dictating two virulent, inept and petty verses about two men who had insulted him during life, G. K. Chesterton and George Moore. Unhappily, they show the side of Hardy which nursed mean grudges, just as much as it retained noble and moving memories, over a whole lifetime.

The chief effect of the complete collection is, however, a more happy one. It shows us how Hardy, though capable from early days of a fine poem in his best manner, 'Neutral Tones' for instance, improved, like Yeats, with the years. Probably his finest single volume now is shown to be the largest, *Moments of Vision*, which came out in 1917 when the poet was seventy-seven years old. It is an astonishing achievement. The poems have acquired, even over those in the previous volume, a new maturity, a symbol of the slow development that Hardy noted in his own personal life. It is partly, of course, that life itself has matured them, with its recent happenings. The death of his wife in late 1912, now fully assimilated, as we have seen, into the most powerful of poetic myths, the further death of his second self, his sister Mary, late in 1915, and the curious secret writing of his concealed autobiography, taking him back over poignant memories of long-past days, have given him a fund of incident, emotion and reflection, on which he can draw for nearly the complete range of human experience. The titles are endless and known to all anthologists, 'The Blinded Bird', 'The Oxen', 'During Wind and Rain', 'Midnight on the Great Western'; but there are a host of others, ever more assured and successful, 'Near Lanivet, 1872', which Hardy significantly thought to be good because it was 'true', 'In the Seventies', 'The Head Above the Fog', 'The Interloper', 'The Five Students' – the list is endless, the achievement startling. So is the improving hand of the poet. The last-named, 'The Five Students', is shown by Gibson (and, in this instance, by Purdy) to have had originally two extra stanzas of commonplace moralising and poetic cliché, which Hardy firmly and wisely cut from the fair copy before it went to the printer. 'On a Heath' had a line which reminds one of the 'University Extension jargon', to which even the loyal Gosse objected in *Jude* – 'in close propinquity' – firmly removed and altered, to leave a moving if still mysterious lyric. James Gibson has shown us a great poet fully at work in his high maturity. All we have to do is to read, to understand, and to marvel.

5 Hardy Among the Poets

Michael Alexander

Prose was his trade, poetry his art, and yet, after fifty years, critics
are still showing us along the beaten track to the monuments of
trade. Our attention is drawn to major novels such as *Jude the Obscure*
and to influences on Hardy's thought, while the bulk of his poetry
remains unread and its worth unestimated. Poets have neglected him
less, and the New Oxford Books of English and of Twentieth Century
English Verse give him greatly enlarged room.[1] Yet while his name is
held in affectionate respect, it does not raise the critical wind that has
blown those of Yeats and Eliot into modern esteem. Notwithstanding
his late *floruit* as a poet (*Poems of 1912–13* is contemporary with
Yeats's *Responsibilities* and Pound's *Lustra*) Hardy remains one of the
Old rather than the Modern Masters.

A memorial essay might aspire to be modest and minute, and could
in any case scarcely affect the cultural predispositions that lead to
Hardy's popular fiction being better known to critics than his poetry.
Yet a few commonplaces and some blunt assertions may indicate
starting-points for the sorting-out and critical estimate that wait to
be undertaken. After which the bearings of the title of this essay
will be pursued more circumspectly.

1. Hardy thought of himself as a poet rather than a novelist.
Victorian England produced better novelists, but the superiority of
another English poet flourishing between 1837 and 1978 would have
to be argued.

2. His position as the last great English poet seems unlikely to be
threatened by Ted Hughes.

3. Whatever the insufficiencies of Hardy's ideas of God, of probability
and of baronets, his verse makes him a dangerous subject for the
kinds of patronage once extended to him as a poor provincial, for
example by James, Eliot and even Leavis.

4. The selections in anthologies, though they have recently improved,
do no kind of justice to his one thousand poems. Though the collected
editions are often muddling, the widespread rumour that most of
Hardy's poems are bad cannot survive any sort of a careful reading.

5. Hardy was not a philosopher. He does not seem even to have

convinced many people that he was, as he claimed to be, a 'meliorist'. His ideas about 'the President of the Immortals' and the 'purblind Doomsters' are not what make him an interesting writer.

6. Hardy was a countryman and a nature poet, and he was born and died in the same parish. Yet he spent a surprising amount of time in London. He had a good schooling, which he improved on, read several languages, travelled, and was something of an antiquarian. He was proficient in music, draughtsmanship and architecture. Though he warbled native woodnotes, he had early learned from William Barnes to do so to Persian and other tunes. He was deeply versed in English poetry. Apart from his well-recorded knowledge of the classics, the Bible and Shakespeare, he was from his first writings deeply indebted to the literature of country life in Wordsworth, and even Gray, as well as Shakespeare. Though partly self-taught, he was in no way a yokel or a naïve genius.

Though this last point may be accepted – and there is no space here to argue the others – it does not banish the image of Hardy as the gloatingly malign rustic pessimist – a distorted image, for which the distortion of his writing career is in part responsible. The circumstances of this career are well enough known, though the following account of it may be less familiar, and I quote it, for, despite its ripeness of manner, it has the right emphases. It comes in Ford Madox Ford's *The March of Literature*; he is engaged in a contrast of Hardy with Whitman.

As an interpreter of our modern day whose motto really is the French peasant's 'La vie, voyez vous, n'est jamais si bonne ni mauvaise que l'on ne croit', Whitman has to stand down before Hardy. Hardy, in fact, was the ideal poet of a generation. He was the most passionate and the most learned of them all. He had the luck, singular in poets, of being able to achieve a competence other than by poetry and then to devote the ending years of his life to his beloved verses. All the while he was making a living and then a competence sufficient to keep him during the closing years of his life, he was, on the side, practising verse-writing, learning the prosodies of every nation that had ever had a prosody. He disliked novel-writing but he made a small fortune by it.

It takes a man with a determination like that to make a great poet. If he has to use that grim determination first to another end, when he is at last released he will write a *Dynasts*.[2]

The novelist's view of Hardy's career is shrewd, and I find a corrective value in the emphases on passion, learning, determination and release. Before the 'release' from prose, Hardy had already stepped out of the shade of the Greenwood Tree, having booby-trapped the Wessex of the endpaper maps with the corpses of Tess and Jude. Wessex-lovers caught sight of a sardonic expression on the mild features, and wondered, with Gosse, what Providence had done to Mr Hardy that he should rise up in the arable land of Wessex and shake his fist at his Creator. This Tolpuddle curmudgeon is not, of course, Thomas Hardy, but the image has stuck. The public could not have expected that a poet should emerge from this septuagenarian chrysalis, especially after *The Dynasts*, nor were his achievements much remarked. Other axes were being noisily ground, and after the war Hardy was a Grand Old Man. His last visit to London was in 1925 (for Harold Macmillan's wedding), by which time modern poetry had usurped the throne.

Yet Providence had played a part in Hardy's career. The publisher's readers to whom *Desperate Remedies* was sent were John Morley and George Meredith; and Alexander Macmillan's letter to Hardy in 1870, though it recommended a cosier tone to the aspiring novelist, is a reminder of nobler days. The timing of Hardy's second début, as poet, was less auspicious; in 1912, according to Ezra Pound, nobody paid any attention to Hardy's verse. In 1908 Ford had founded the *English Review*, in order, as he quixotically claimed, to print a poem which Hardy could not get published anywhere in England. The *English Review* marvellously united the old and the new writers in a way that was soon to become impossible; it is important on the present occasion to recognise that Hardy also united the old and the new. His presence has haunted almost all subsequent English poets, and it can now be seen that the modern English poetic tradition flowed, or oozed wistlessly, through him.

This may seem improbable. In 'An Ancient to Ancients' Hardy wrote:

> The bower we shrined to Tennyson,
>> Gentlemen,
> Is roof-wrecked, damps there drip upon
> Sagged seats, the creeper-nails are rust,
> The spider is sole denizen.

The rhyme alone might seem to disqualify him from being a hander-on of anything, yet Pound, for example, a blithe bower-wrecker, had the deepest respect for Hardy and expressed it throughout his career. His retrospect of 1964 is particularly apposite; I reproduce a few of his dicta: 'No man ever had so much Latin and so eschewed the least appearance of being a classicist on the surface.' 'Contemporary for a long time with Browning on whom he improves at his, Hardy's,

c

best, taking over the marrow of the tradition . . .' 'No one trying to learn writing in regular, formed verse can learn better than in observing what Thomas Hardy accepted from Browning and what he pruned away from his more busteous or rambunctious predecessor.' 'Nobody, on occasion, ever used rhyme with less insult to statement. . . .' 'The poems of 1912–13 lift him to his apex, sixteen poems from "The Going" to "Castle Boterel", all good, and enough for a lifetime. "The Waterfall" is the lead-up, at the end of the volume just precedent.' Thinking about Hardy's comment on his own *Homage to Sextus Propertius*, Pound is struck by 'the degree in which Hardy would have had his mind on the SUBJECT MATTER, and how little he cared about manner, which does not in the least mean that he did not care about it or had not a definite aim.'[3]

The remarks on Latin, metre, rhyme, on Browning and subject-matter, are not, from Pound, surprising. More notable here are the stresses on 'the tradition' and on the *Poems of 1912–13*. I suggest later in this essay that Hardy, countrified rhymester though he may have seemed through Vorticist spectacles, conformed before it was articulated to Pound's demand for 'direct treatment of the object' – the 'natural object' which, in Pound's view, was 'the proper and perfect symbol'.[4]

I also find it helpful to see Hardy as carrying on not only the dramatic tradition of Browning, but the main lyric tradition of the expression of personal emotion, within which Browning is a variant, as well as the deeper pastoral bias in English poetry going back beyond Wordsworth. Or, as Ford put it, concluding his comparison with Whitman in his most Corinthian manner for the benefit of his American audience:

> He had a peasant intelligence; so he was wise. He resembled the root of a four-hundred-year-old tree; he resembled a moss-covered rock that has lain for four hundred years in a forest. So he knew that destiny attends on chance since chance is always characteristic of the circumstances in which it takes part. Beside him, Whitman was an hysteriac. He was not wise. The essential townsman can never be wise because he cannot see life for the buildings. Whitman saw factories rise and was excited over the future of the race. Hardy saw factories smudge his rural scene, and was merely depressed. He knew that the human heart remained the essential stamping ground of the poet.[5]

If T. S. Eliot had a stamping ground it may indeed have been the human heart, but he made it known that he did not stamp there personally. He had, in an extreme form, the reserve that made Hardy say, in the preface to *Wessex Poems*: 'the pieces are in a large degree dramatic and personative in conception: and this even where they are not obviously so.' Yet Eliot recoiled from the directness with which Hardy dealt with 'personative' emotional situations that were also transparently personal. In the wake of Eliot's impersonal strategy for poetry, with its associated irony, ambiguity and symbolic complexity, modern critics have found little to say about poetry which is not complex in this way. As Pound noted, 'When a writer's matter is stated with such entirety and with such clarity there is no place left for the explaining critic.' The 'matter' Hardy 'states' is not primarily English country life – the background of his novels and earlier verse – but the emotional realities of individual lives.

Considering the expression of powerful feeling in poetry, one cannot evade Wordsworth, though in their reforming criticism Eliot and Pound treat his name as taboo. It is interesting, then, to find Pound reproducing, from Hardy's Prefatory Apology to *Late Lyrics and Earlier* (1922), the passage from Wordsworth's *Preface* rebutting the supposition 'that by the act of writing in verse an author makes a formal engagement that he will gratify certain known habits of association: that he not only thus apprises the reader that certain classes of ideas and expressions will be found in his book, but that others will be carefully excluded.' Hardy's Apology also invokes the phrases 'obstinate questionings' and 'blank misgivings', taking it for granted that the reader will know their source in the Immortality Ode. He later calls on Wordsworth a third time. Indeed, the inclusion of unwonted 'ideas and expressions' in his verse is only one aspect of Hardy's allegiance to Wordsworth. If Crabbe invented peasant tragedy, Wordsworth ennobled it, and Hardy chose it as his first stamping ground. The endurance of elemental feeling in 'natural' lives is the presupposition of all his work: Gabriel Oak, as both his names suggest, is a matinée version of Wordsworth's Michael. Hardy says that in his youth Wordsworth was the norm of poetry, and indeed his first poem, 'Domicilium', is steeped in Wordsworth, both in its verse and its feeling. The machinery and melodrama of Hardy's tales, though like *Michael* they are related 'For the delight of a few natural hearts', weakens them; but the best of his poems are worthy of his allegiance. The *Poems of 1912–13* are in the tradition created by the Lucy poems, particularly 'A slumber did my spirit seal'. The personal loss is less concealed, more narrowly autobiographical, but the poet's personal experience is raised into a representative myth – which is the essence of Wordsworth's development of the English poetic tradition. Again, the source of Hardy's imagery is predominantly 'the natural object', or complex of natural objects, to which

Wordsworth ultimately returns, as in the celebrated passage on the restoration of the imagination in Book XIII of the *Prelude*:

> The single sheep and the one blasted tree,
> And the bleak music from that old stone wall.

To be sure, one does not imagine Hardy, on his bicycle, 'grasping at a wall or a tree to recall himself from the abyss of idealism to the reality', or not so frequently as Wordsworth; for all his ghosts and his moments of vision, he has a more literal eye – and a more exactly specific turn of phrase. For Hardy the milk 'purrs into the pail', the morning 'hardens against the wall' – one is aware that these are impinging on the privacy of a highly idiosyncratic consciousness, that it is a Thomas Hardy who records this. But his poetry, like Wordsworth's, moves from observation and description to a more generally symbolic presentation. The relative ease and informality both of Hardy's natural observation, and of the ways in which he invests it with significance, are due in part to the speeding-up of expressive conventions established by Wordsworth.

'An August Midnight' may furnish some evidence to test these large suggestions:

I

> A shaded lamp and a waving blind,
> And the beat of a clock from a distant floor:
> On this scene enter – winged, horned, and spined –
> A longlegs, a moth, and a dumbledore;
> While 'mid my page there idly stands
> A sleepy fly, that rubs its hands . . . .

II

> Thus meet we five, in this still place,
> At this point of time, at this point in space.
> – My guests besmear my new-penned line,
> Or bang at the lamp and fall supine.
> 'God's humblest, they!' I muse. Yet why?
> They know Earth-secrets that know not I.

The observation here is more casual, minute, even trivial, than Wordsworth's, and might at first seem not far from Yeats's parody of a modern poem: 'I am sitting in a chair, there are three dead flies on a corner of the ceiling.' Yet its particularity does not reflect a vacancy. There is a dramatic novelist's skill in the scene-setting; then the distracted eye focuses on to the hands of this unlikely Hamlet;

and the mind floats out to consider time and space. The musing that follows might strike an unaccustomed reader as overcondensed, or a blasé reader as sententious and even morbid. Yet Hardy believed that 'unadjusted impressions have their value', and the musing has dramatic congruity. It may be that the moral (an intimation of mortality) is not quite adequate to all the alarms set off by 'At this point of time, at this point in space'. Even this inadequacy may be seen as Wordsworthian. More clearly in the tradition of Wordsworth is the diapason from tiny and transient to mortal and cosmic – as with the violet and the star in 'She dwelt among untrodden ways' – and, again, the way the tables are turned on the writer, his realisation that his initial reading is quite outflanked by a bleaker natural reality. There are many differences – no immortality here – and this is a slight piece, but the ancestry of the mode of the poem is not in doubt. Hardy's particularity and queerness do not make the pattern of the poem, the way it develops its symbolic extension, different in kind from the Wordsworthian model.

Tributary influences on Hardy's tradition are the dramatic, from Browning, and the narrative, and these complicate the inheritance. Eliot's charge that Hardy is self-absorbed (again, not unlike Wordsworth) overlooks the detachment with which Hardy notes events that impinge on his consciousness; it also neglects his 'personative' ability – seen in 'we five' – to enter into the viewpoint of persons, animals and natural forces at points in time and space very different from his own. Several early poems are called 'She, to Him', 'He, to Her'; others take the different corners of emotional triangles, or tell more tangled tales. This develops later into an ability to dramatise and embody his own predicaments, and also to give them a narrative rather than a merely expressive interest. In *Poems of 1912–13* Hardy presents himself as a character in a drama, almost like an Elizabethan. This set of poems is the easiest extended text to take from the poems as they are arranged at the moment; and one of the most important of them, 'After a Journey', may serve as a familiar example to try out some of these suggestions.

The death of his first wife, Emma Lavinia, took place on 27 November 1912, at which point in Hardy's notebook we find: 'Sent £20 to the Pension Fund, Society of Authors, making £25 in all.'[6] We know that the marriage had not turned out happily – 'Summer gave us sweets, but autumn wrought division' – and that Emma's death revived with astonishing force the ardour of Hardy's early love. The 1912–13 poems (and many others on the same subject) are poems of love as well as loss. The epigraph, *veteris vestigia flammae*, is a well-known tag from the opening of the fourth book of the *Aeneid*, yet poignantly apt. The widowed Dido recognises the traces of the long-quenched flame of passion now rekindled by the sight and story of Aeneas. The bereaved Hardy is likewise consumed by the painful memories aroused by all the vestiges of Emma – memories of disappointment mixed with guilt, which he seeks to appease by retracing his *footsteps* ('Down the years, down the dead scenes I have tracked you') to the scenes of their courtship in Cornwall in March 1870. 'After a Journey' begins 'Hereto I come to view a voiceless ghost' – a ghost which appears in several of the poems, and not unlike the ghost of Dido encountered by Aeneas in Hades.

This journey back to 'Lyonnesse' is inscribed in the memorable landscape of the early romance, *A Pair of Blue Eyes* (1873). Hardy's later preface to the book, dated March 1895, ends:

> The place is pre-eminently (for one person at least) the region of dream and mystery. The ghostly birds, the pall-like sea, the frothy wind, the eternal soliloquy of the waters, the bloom of dark purple cast, that seems to exhale from the shoreward precipices, in themselves lend to the scene an atmosphere like the twilight of a night vision.
>
> One enormous sea-bord cliff in particular figures in the narrative; and for some forgotten reason or other this cliff was described in the story as being without a name. Accuracy would require the statement to be that a remarkable cliff which resembles in many points the cliff of the description bears a name that no event has made famous.

This is Beeny Cliff, revisited in March 1913, as the poem of that title relates, and the scene also of 'After a Journey' and 'At Castle Boterel'. Hardy had earlier written 'The shore and country about Castle Boterel . . . is the furthest westward of all those convenient corners wherein I have ventured to erect my theatre for these imperfect little dramas of country life and passions.' Like some of his less imperfect ones, *A Pair of Blue Eyes* contains great scenes, in one of which Hardy contrives that Knight, an amateur geologist, hanging by his fingernails from the top of Beeny Cliff, should find himself face to face with the fossil of a Trilobite; whereupon 'Time closed up like a fan before him. He saw himself at one extremity of the years, face to face with the beginning and all the intermediate centuries simultaneously.'[7]

Again and again in *Poems of 1912–13* Time closes up like a fan, though by means of conjunctions and coincidences less contrived than in the romances and most of the novels. Hardy's little dramas move from scene to scene, and in the romances the links between them are perfunctory, for the scenes exist to set up the 'moments of vision' that they embody; these moments of vision are remarkable for their subjective intensity, their feeling of fatality, not for their circumstantial probability or objective necessity. Thus at the beginning of *Two on a Tower* there is a chance fatality about Lady Constantine's wish to visit the tower; or of Elfride's wish to walk around the top of another tower in *A Pair of Blue Eyes*; or about Gabriel Oak's presence at the haystack fire. In later novels the concatenation is riveted more carefully, so that Tess's choice, led up to by a series of forced choices, determines the rest of her life. These fatal conjunctions are hung, sometimes unhappily, on a temporal sequence; and the more characters, the more obvious the scaffolding of chance.

In poetry Hardy could dispense with the temporal sequence and the furniture of novels and still have the concentrated character-revelations at moments of crisis, for the sake of which his narratives were constructed. Hence the superiority of the poetry: the novels crank themselves up to dramatic situations whereas the poems grow out of them. The dramatic or personative poems can begin in the middle of the meeting and work outwards, backwards or forwards in time. Hardy's eye for place and scene allows him to create firmly and economically the background which produces the unique moment. In the novels, the firmness of the scene-setting often contrasts strangely with the shakiness of the plot-machinery. In Hardy the presence and energy of places – 'interlune' on Egdon Heath, for example – can convincingly determine the action of persons. This energy between places and persons is generated in a neater and more controlled form in the poems, as in 'An August Midnight'; in his own experience and under the stress of his own emotions, Hardy had no need to manufacture artificially dramatic situations. The sleepy fly appears more naturally than the Trilobite.

Theatre conventions, however, remain useful to Hardy in his later poetry. 'After a Journey', for example, can be described in theatrical terms: 'Enter poet, advance stage front, addresses audience, turns to wife's ghost, addresses it indirectly, questions it directly.' Stanza two contains her imagined reply. There are also stage-directions: 'up and down', 'facing round about me everywhere', 'leading me on', 'I now fraily follow', 'here' and 'here'. Time and place appear very naturally and vividly, and the poem owes much of its immediacy and authenticity to the practised ease with which Hardy deploys these conventions, themselves as old as the Shakespearian soliloquy – 'Is this a dagger that I see before me', for example, contains all necessary indications of gesture and movement. Equally stage-hallowed is the convention that the voiceless ghost, besought to speak, shows the courting place, and must disappear before dawn.

The apostrophes and rhetorical questions, the 'answers' and the final protestation are likewise traditional, even stagy, but appear natural. Such conventions articulate and dramatise what would otherwise be mere autobiographical utterance, and we eavesdrop on Hardy's colloquy with his dead wife without feeling its improbability.

This self-dramatisation – 'Yes: I have re-entered your olden haunts at last' – is rescued from melodrama by the specific way in which the night landscape and its visitor are realised, both in its actual detail and in his idiosyncratic perception of it; thus 'soliloquies' was revised to 'ejaculations', 'viewed' to 'scanned'. Equally precise and peculiar to Hardy's eye and locution are 'nut-coloured hair', 'there's no knowing', 'wherein' and the extraordinary

> Ignorant of what there is flitting here to see,
> The waked birds preen and the seals flop lazily.

The credible, authentic and particular coexist in the poem, however, with the general, the eloquent, the Shakespearian, as in 'Time's derision', 'Life lours' and, especially, her imagined words and his closing declaration. Here we touch the critical problem of Hardy's diction and style, never adequately described. Too much has been made of his oddness or inelegance, not enough of his strength and eloquence. Much of his language is idiomatic everyday speech: 'the spots we knew', 'the cave just under', 'I am just the same'. Yet he easily and unselfconsciously uses the traditional language of poetry: 'olden haunts', 'twain', 'Time', and, quaintly, 'the stars close their shutters'. Both ordinary and poetic speech are used firmly, even roughly, unaesthetically, and what is literary in his style is old, absorbed, time-honoured. Not that Hardy lacks finesse – *haunted* in line 18 is perfectly calculated – but he deliberately avoided the appearance of finish, he concealed his art; his wood needed no veneer. Not that Hardy is a *plain* writer: he certainly works nearer the staple of English than, say, Hopkins, but on the other hand he is capable of the (entirely successful) grand rhetoric of 'Beeny Cliff'.

The genuineness of the feeling in 'After a Journey', the lack of sentimentality even in his gallant final sentiment, has made it admired, and this must be due to its solidity and simplicity: it unfolds from a single impulse. We are moved partly because we are so clearly and specifically presented with what it is that we are to be moved by; and we believe in Hardy as a character and in the reality of his world. Given the eloquence to which he can rise, as at the end, this may seem enough. It could be argued, however, that this is successful dramatisation of an essentially private emotion – a remark-

able achievement but still a limited, individual one. Such I take it is
Eliot's objection, recently raised again by Donald Davie.[8]

I believe that, within his realistic mode of presentation, Hardy
successfully invests his experience with wider meaning. Where he
strives to provide symbols for the larger entities who have to stand
in for an absent God, as in *The Dynasts* and other cosmic fables, he
is normally not successful, and I am surprised to see anthologists
preferring such poems. Apart from Father Time in *Jude*, he does not
characteristically go in for symbols in the way of Ibsen or Lawrence:
if Egdon Heath, or the Shearing Barn, or, say, the Darkling Thrush
are symbols, they are simple, innocent and effective. He does not
essay the more refined, flexible and enigmatic symbolism of Chekhov.
Indeed, he is not a conscious symbolist at all: it is more his way to
begin with the local, actual and particular and to arrange them so
as to bring out a natural meaning and significance which can,
however, achieve a much more universal resonance than is suggested
by dwelling on his idiosyncratic language and observant eye. Less of
an idealist and more of a sceptic than Wordsworth, his secularised
religious feeling finds its way back into awe at the universe and its
inhabitants.

This feeling for the presences in Man, in Nature and in Human Life,
far more than the avowed pessimism, meliorism, Darwinism or determinism which war with it, is Hardy's underlying religion; and it
is for this that he is read – an unofficial trust in the imagination,
which, alongside his realistic bleakness, reaffirms his inheritance from
Wordsworth. For all his conscientious clutches at positivism, he at
last remained mercifully unconfined by the advanced ideas of his day.

This awe or unofficial imagination gives his realism the resonance
to raise it beyond the interest attaching to an individual's 'unadjusted
impressions' of three dead flies on a corner of the ceiling. Though
Hardy consciously renounces the vague glamour and consolations of
ideal and symbolic systems, his sensibility is permeated by them.
The empirical modern English poet, his successor, has likewise for-
sworn the heroic imaginative codes of Yeats and Eliot, but cannot do
without them. Again, Pound's precepts for modern poetry, where they
are not merely technical, are realist and even positivist in their
assumptions: but he too remained a transcendentalist at heart.

The third stanza of 'After a Journey' may serve as example of
what Wordsworth calls a fair train of imagery. The waterfall, the
mist-bow, the cave and the voice all seem to me exactly the kind of
natural symbols that Pound asked for, though more solid and
traditional than his own early choices. All, apart from the 'voice',
are actual phenomena. All, like the word 'haunted', possess a latent
symbolic suggestion, not forced upon us but activated by the con-

text. The waterfall may suggest beauty, passion and transience, the mist-bow a hope with some fragility, the cave oracular prophecy. Yet each remains itself and does not become an emblem.

The association of ambiguous oracular prophecy with the cave might seem too classical to be likely in Hardy, were it not that the 'voice' is 'hollow' and its echoes are redoubled in 'ago', 'aglow', and 'follow'. A mist-bow is not a rainbow, and may likewise seem a natural phenomenon here, without a literary or a classical association. But, in the closely related 'Beeny Cliff', we find that over the lovers 'there flew an *irised* rain'. It may be that as, for Hardy, life and love flattered only to deceive, rainbows should suggest to him delusive hope. (It may even be in his mind that at the end of *Aeneid* IV it is Iris who cuts the thread of Dido's life in which case an analogy with Aeneas and Dido might be conscious, and the cave would also suggest love, sin and betrayal.) The waterfall is, clearly, just a waterfall; any suggestions of beauty and transience are entirely natural. The poem Pound picked out, 'Under the Waterfall', makes it explicit that for Hardy this waterfall directly symbolised the high romance of his courtship. This ingenuously symbolic poem, which is partly in doggerel, tells us that the waterfall was 'About three spans wide and two spans tall', which may or may not be a sincere form of flattery, but certainly shows a Wordsworthian baldness of style and acceptance of 'the natural object'. It begins:

> Whenever I plunge my arm, like this,
> In a basin of water, . . .

So the waterfall, mist-bow and cave provided a magic and a secluded place for the lovers' picnic forty years before, and now, in the haunted night, form a complex symbol both of promise and of hollowness. But the 'then fair hour' and the 'hollow' voice are the only pointers to remoter symbolic associations of mist-bows or voices from caves, and the success of the stanza does not depend on such recognitions. Hardy's symbolism, then, is latent, unassertive, optional. His urgent juxtaposition of the fairness of 'then' and the frailty of 'now', and his success at conveying what in 'Places' he calls the 'beneaped and stale' quality of quotidian experience, exemplified here in the heavy ignorance of the flopping seals, indicates that he conversely wished to invest the 'then fair hour' with all the symbolic radiance and splendour of Wordsworth's Immortality Ode.

'Afterwards' is often anthologised, and its imagery provides a final example of Hardy's modulation of natural description into symbolic suggestion. In it Hardy wonders whether after he is dead the sight of natural things will recall him to the minds of those who knew him.

Many poems bear witness to his concern that the dead are soon quite forgotten – the second death, he calls it – and he was a great frequenter of churchyards. The English have traditionally domesticated the classical preoccupation with immortality and fame in their country churchyards; Gray's *Elegy* supplied Hardy with much more than the title of *Far from the Madding Crowd*. Hardy once said that it would have been possible for Wordsworth to see him in his cradle, as for Thomas Gray to have seen Wordsworth in his. This choice of fairy godfathers is revealing, as, ever since Wordsworth disliked Gray's poetic diction, we are used to connecting the artificial *Elegy* with *Lycidas* or *The Scholar Gypsy*, and a natural poem like 'Afterwards' with Wordsworth. But Hardy, like Gray, was interested in fame and obscurity as well as in graves.

I have long thought that the *Elegy* may have contributed to 'Afterwards', especially from the quatrains that so moved Johnson ('For who to dumb forgetfulness a prey') to the end. Particularly apposite to the query repeated in the refrain of 'Afterwards' is Gray's imagined interview between 'some kindred spirit' and 'some hoary-headed swain':

> For thee who, mindful of the unhonoured dead,
> Dost in these lines their artless tale relate;
> If chance, by lonely Contemplation led,
> Some kindred spirit shall inquire thy fate,
>
> Haply some hoary-headed swain may say,
> 'Oft have we seen him at the peep of dawn
> Brushing with hasty steps the dews away
> To meet the sun upon the upland lawn. . . .'

The conventional pastoral scenes where the swain missed the youth are quite different in purpose from Hardy's realistic vignettes, but their pattern is similar, and one or two details have tiny echoes – 'customed'/'customary'; 'upland lawn'/'upland thorn'. The epitaph which Gray sympathetically provides for himself contains the lines:

> Fair Science frowned not on his humble birth
> And Melancholy marked him for her own.

They eminently apply to the creator of *Jude the Obscure*.

Each stanza of 'Afterwards' asks the same question in a slightly different way, and the poem deepens as the relation of refrain to stanza develops. The elaborate fine image of the first stanza is flattened by the mundane tone of 'Will the neighbours say . . .'. This ordinariness, found again in 'must have been a familiar sight' and the slight bathos of the hedgehog stanza, is eventually purged by the power of the images, and the 'unadjusted' refrains lose their apparent clumsiness. This strain between the mundane and the transcendent is a calculated effect.

Consideration of the imagery discloses the changing backgrounds of a day in May, a summer dusk, a dark summer night, a clear winter night, and, finally, an unspecified gloom. The leading image of each stanza is, in turn, a butterfly, a hawk, a hedgehog, stars, the bell. The processes of a parish, a countryside and a whole year seem to be brought in to the poem. Hardy's mild hope that he will be remembered as a man who used to notice such things fades under the inclusiveness of this revolving cycle of life and death : the butterfly and hedgehog are prey to the larger agencies of the hawk, the bell and the stars, and we are kindred to them. This kinship is suggested by subtle relationships in the imagery : the arrival of the ephemeral wings and leaves of May hints also at the tremulous departure of the soul from its chrysalis; the ominous hawk 'crosses the shades'; the hedgehog's transit is mortal, the neighbours 'stand at the door' to say farewell, but also to leave; their thoughts 'rise' on them as the stars rise into the sky. Everything in the world of the poem is intrinsicate.

The last stanza, particularly the line 'Till they rise again, as they were a new bell's boom', raises in acute form the possibility that the imagery of the poem, so far from being leaves from a country-lover's notebook, has a consistent symbolic dimension involving metaphors of a sort not to be expected from a naturalist, still less an atheist. Mythical and classical literature provide many associations for the figures Hardy employs in the poem : if the hawk and the hedgehog suggest a Darwinian mortality, the butterfly, the stars and the bell suggest, respectively, the immortality of the soul, stellification and resurrection. There are suggestions that death is final ('he is gone', 'he hears it not now'); that it is a change of form ('stilled'); and even that it is the prelude to immortality (stanzas 1 and 5). The pragmatic neighbours of stanza 1 fade away, via 'a gazer', 'one' and 'those', to 'any', whereas the *things* remain, and the certainty of 'he hears it not now' hangs rather thinly in the air. Agnostic and sceptical though it is, 'Afterwards' is not good evidence that Hardy believed that there was no afterlife. The impotence prosaically expressed in stanza 3 is followed by the exaltation of stanza 4 and the enigmatic hints of stanza 5. The irony of the last line includes the neighbours, just as in the last line of 'The Darkling Thrush' it includes the poet.

Over the page from 'Afterwards' is the Apology, where Hardy rebuts the attribution to him of 'a view of life', claiming that the 'said "view" ' was really 'a series of fugitive impressions which I have never tried to coordinate.' With one or two exceptions, this seems to me quite fair, certainly as a comment on 'Afterwards'. (It is to be followed later by a complimentary reference to Cardinal Newman.) If, as Davie says, Hardy's example has been so important to recent English poetry, the intellectual and emotional shortcomings of that poetry are not to be found in Hardy, despite his positivism and liberalism, for in his poetry these are subverted by something far more deeply interfused.

I have suggested that Hardy's poetry has a modern as well as a traditional aspect, recognised at the time by Pound. It is clear that he is the last *English* poet that English poets have felt able to look back to with confidence. He has enjoyed the high esteem of such very different poets as Lawrence, Graves, Auden, Betjeman, Davie and Larkin. Many active English poets apart from Larkin have rejected the experimental and intellectual poetry that now seems historically associated with international modernism, and are no happier with the extremism of the confessional, surreal or expressionist schools. Hardy is honest with personal experience, and is the last major English practitioner of autobiographical poetry in a traditional form. His technical skill and restraint are the formal counterparts to the stoicism and reserve with which he treats his emotions. It would be pleasant to be able to record that English reluctance to join the modern movement had been accompanied by an imaginative use of English poetic traditions, or by the practice of those skills of versification which are perhaps Hardy's most available legacy.

NOTES

1 In the *New Oxford Book of English Verse* only Shakespeare and Wordsworth are given a greater number of poems than Hardy, although several other poets get more pages. In the *Oxford Book of Twentieth Century English Verse*, Larkin gives Hardy more poems than anyone else, and only Eliot has more pages.

2 *The March of Literature* (London, 1939), pp. 707–8 (first U.S. edition, 1938).

3 *Confucius to Cummings*, ed. Ezra Pound and Marcella Spann (New York, 1964), pp. 325–8. For Hardy's importance to Pound, see Donald Davie's third chapter in *Pound* (London, 1975), and John Peck, 'Pound and Hardy', *Agenda*, x, 2–3, which also has Davie's fine piece, 'Hardy's Virgilian Purples'.

4 *Literary Essays of Ezra Pound*, ed. T. S. Eliot (London, 1954), 'A Retrospect' (1918), p. 9.

5 Op. cit., p. 708.

6 *Thomas Hardy's Notebooks*, ed. Evelyn Hardy (London, 1955), p. 74.

7 *A Pair of Blue Eyes*, Wessex Edition (London, 1916), ch. XXII, p. 253.

8 In *Thomas Hardy and English Poetry* (London, 1974).

6 Some Thoughts on Hardy and Religion

T. R. M. Creighton

'In essence all living things – including man – are the result of a purely accidental and unpredictable biochemical "situation" which produces the succeeding genetic mutation. In short man is an accident based on *chance* and the accident is perpetuated by the *necessity* of chemical reactions . . . in a universe without causality.' This is the summary given on the jacket of a recent work by an authoritative evolutionary geneticist, Professor Jacques Monod.[1] I don't suppose such a statement causes any holder of any religious belief, whether institutional, independent, esoteric or anything else – and it is surprising how many there are today even in the scientifically enlightened West – any trouble at all. We shall have a look at the reasons why later. Monod's conclusion, whether true or false, was inherent in scientific investigation from its inception; for if something outside nature exists – the supernatural, God or whatever name you like to give to what has been the object of man's religious impulse since he 'first emerged from the den of time'[2] – it will not be discovered by inquiry into nature; and if it is only the product of imagination, it will not be discovered anyhow. It will not be found by looking at what natural science cannot yet explain. 'There are reverent minds who ceaselessly scan the fields of nature and the books of science in search of gaps – gaps which they fill up with God. As if God lived in gaps.' So Henry Drummond wrote in *The Ascent of Man* in 1894.

Monod's conclusion was comprehended in terms of natural science in Darwin's theory of evolution, though Darwin and his fellow-scientists in the nineteenth century were very cautious about stating the full implications of the theory whether they perceived them or not. Some poets perceived the full implications of scientific inquiry very early and enunciated them much more vigorously than the scientists did – Tennyson, though he claims to have rejected it on the grounds of the primacy of feeling, expresses Monod's view of the universe perfectly in many cantos of *In Memoriam*, written before *The Origin of Species* had appeared. Hardy perceived the same necessary intellectual consequences of scientific theory in the 1860s when he was in his twenties, and stated them forcibly and with apparent conviction in the sonnet 'Hap', written in 1866. There is, he says, no God, not even a 'vengeful' one, no intelligent direction of the universe; 'crass casualty' (which later he glossed as 'insensible chance') controls everything. But whereas to the modern scientific rationalist this conclusion is emotionally neutral – if anything it is to be welcomed because science has proved it true and it will lead to a true humanism, 'the development of an ethic of knowledge that will save man'[3] – to Hardy in 1866 it was emotionally repugnant and quite unacceptable. It showed that human life, which he had learnt in his Dorset childhood was lived under and sanctified by divine providence, whatever occasional suffering and evil the sin of Adam and the fall of man might entail, was not this at all but a purely tragic process. Man had no eternal destiny but was the doomed being he increasingly appears to be in the great novels culminating in *Jude*, whose hopes exist only to be frustrated and whose ambitions are idle dreams. Life was purposeless and meaningless – 'the progress of mortals through a world not worthy of them'.[4]

When Hardy was seventeen, his chief religious preoccupation had been with the relative merits of infant and adult baptism and 'though he was appalled by the feebleness of the arguments for infant christening . . . he incontinently determined to "stick to his own side" as he considered the Church to be, at some costs of conscience.'[5] In 1865 he wrote in his diary: 'July 5. Sunday. To Westminster Abbey morning service. Stayed to the Sacrament. A very odd experience amid a crowd of strangers.' In 1866 he wrote 'Hap'. It is a rapid and puzzling progression.

In the 1860s Hardy read *The Origin of Species*, *Essays and Reviews*, and much else that they may be taken to represent, and *Poems and Ballads* for which alone, as a poet, he expressed enthusiasm as well as admiration. They burst upon him

> as though a garland of red roses
> Had fallen about the hood of some smug nun

in 'Victoria's formal middle time'. And he suffered what is commonly called 'Victorian loss of faith', though the term is a misleading one and loss of *belief* describes the experience much better. Faith in its true sense is the feeling Hopkins had about the universe and Hardy and most other Victorians did not – a supra-rational, intuitive sense of a divine being which, whether you like to regard it as a particu-

larly dotty psychological delusion or a supreme insight into the
nature of things vouchsafed to only a very few in any generation,
is not lost through acquaintance with *The Origin of Species* and the
rest, and is not vulnerable by logical arguments or emotional impressions which seem to contradict it. We know from various entries
in the *Note-books and Papers* and from the 'Andromeda' sonnet that
Hopkins was just as aware as his contemporary Hardy of the
objections to Christian belief current in their time and that he had
at least as fastidious and rigorous an intellect, but scientific facts had
none of the relevance to his faith that they had to Hardy's belief
and did nothing to shake it. The final upshot of his work, if one
considers the last sonnets, is more tragic than that of all Hardy's
multifarious dealings with religion, but the tragic conflict takes place
on a different plane, as it were on a different wavelength. Hopkins'
God who

> Wert thou my enemy, O thou my friend,
> How couldst thou more, I wonder, than thou dost
> Defeat, thwart me?

and to whom his laments were

> cries countless, cries like dead letters sent
> To dearest him that lives alas! away

has no connection with the God whom Hardy lost in the 1860s and
of whom he wrote just before his fiftieth birthday: 'I have been
looking for God for fifty years and I think that if he had existed I
should have discovered him. As an external personality, of course –
the only true meaning of the word.'[6] Hopkins in all his sufferings –
'my fire and fever fussy' – had kept his faith; Hardy had had, and
then lost, belief. Of course Hopkins' faith was heavily dependent on
the Roman Catholic Church, the Jesuit Order and the *Spiritual
Exercises*. But he had gone out to look for them, chosen them as
the necessary vehicle for his faith; they were not a hereditary
possession. Hardy was born into the primitive High Anglicanism he
learnt at his mother's knee ānd in Stinsford church – he inherited
and did not choose it and what his emotions found indispensable
throughout life, though his intellect and reason found themselves
bound to reject it, was much more the institutional quality of the
church, its doctrines, architecture and music, its traditions and
personal associations and even the superstitions it harboured than
any intuitive faith or conception of a divine being. No falser estimate
of Hardy has ever been given than Eliot's: 'a powerful personality

uncurbed by any institutional attachment or by submission to any objective beliefs.'

It was just Hardy's institutional attachment to the Anglican Church and his emotional feeling for its beliefs that produced his religious dilemma, the rift between his feelings and his intellect which is the most fundamental and fructifying element in his art. His emotions were pious rather than in any original way devotional or mystical. He needed a religious belief, an explanation of the universe in supernatural terms, more desperately than most men do. Many possibilities of undogmatic, non-institutional Christian belief were opening up during his lifetime – Tolstoy's revolutionary Christianity for instance, the whole line of thinking which emanated from Kierkegaard, Schweitzer's Christian agnosticism and much else. And there were other religions such as the Buddhism which later on nearly claimed Eliot. It was less, I suggest, the rigour of his intellect than his institutional attachment to the Church that prevented him from ever entertaining any freer, looser expression of his religious impulses, that kept him wandering in the deserts between Darwin and Jehovah instead of exploring any of their oases.

The religious situation has changed so much that it is almost impossible for anyone today, certainly for any young person, to enter into this experience of loss of belief as it occurred to someone of Hardy's generation. For one thing, however strong a religious belief a child may inherit from his family, and even if he continues to hold it fervently, he cannot in our world reach adulthood without encountering many scientific and rationalistic objections to belief – at least the theory of evolution and some of its consequences – and recognising that he lives in a predominantly secular and unbelieving age. No one can be suddenly confronted as Hardy was in his twenties by rationalism and science. For another, religion is no longer a cohesive and generally accepted social force. The Church of England, which almost everyone formally belonged to, respected and visited, held the Dorset of Hardy's boyhood together and even dissenters or Roman Catholics were regarded with mild suspicion. Today the most committed believer knows that a majority of people just as respectable as his own family, living in the same town, street or village, do not share his traditional belief and probably have none at all. To find an analogue to 'Higher Bockhampton in the parish of Stinsford, Dorset', as it was in the 1840s one has to look to the Muslim world – say to a village in Hausaland in northern Nigeria where the whole community subscribes to the same beliefs, even if many of its members transgress its commandments in their personal behaviour, heeds the same calls to prayer and participates in the same rituals.

Though Hardy lost his belief in the doctrines of the Church of

England, he continued to look to it for social coherence and to the religious impulse as essential to civilised life. I quote at length a passage from the 'Apology' to *Late Lyrics and Earlier*, written in 1922, because it so well illustrates Hardy's emotional need and intellectual confusion in matters of religion. The analytically-minded reader will detect the bad logic, the vague definition of words like 'religion', 'rationality' and 'poetry', and the visionary impossibility of the whole proposal which lies behind the appearance of restrained passion in the prose.

> What other purely English establishment than the Church, of sufficient dignity and footing, with such strength of old association, such scope for transmutability, such architectural spell, is left in this country to keep the shreds of morality together? It may indeed be a forlorn hope, a mere day-dream of an alliance between religion, which must be retained unless the world is to perish, and complete rationality, which must come unless also the world is to perish, by means of the interfusing effect of poetry. But . . . I repeat that I forlornly hope so notwithstanding the supercilious regard of hope by Schopenhauer, von Hartmann, and other philosophers down to Einstein who have my respect.

No one could hold such a hope in the world today.

A third obstacle to our entering into Hardy's experience is that the war between science and religion is over. Each has learnt to respect – or to disregard – the other as parallel discourses which 'though infinite, can never meet'.[7] Many people can accommodate both discourses simultaneously. As David Lack writes, today 'there are theologians who accept the findings of biologists in the evolutionary field, while among evolutionary biologists of repute there are not only atheists and agnostics, but Unitarians, Quakers, Methodists, Presbyterians, Anglicans and Roman Catholics who hold their divergent views with strong conviction and apparent integrity. This suggests, at least, that the problem is not simple.'[8] Such accommodation was rarer in the nineteenth century. Charles Kingsley could write: 'Science is the Voice of God – her facts, His words – to which we must each and all reply "Speak, Lord, for thy servants heareth" '; but the official attitude of the Church was obscurantist and hostile both to science, as at the famous Oxford meeting of the British Association in 1858, and to attempts to modify the rigidity of its supernatural assertions as we see from its reception of *Essays and Reviews* and its treatment of men like F. D. Maurice and Bishop Colenso. And though Huxley could write 'the doctrine of evolution is neither Anti-Theistic nor Theistic. It simply has no more to do with Theism than the first book of Euclid', the growing resentment of scientists at what seemed the arrogance of the Church is better reflected in Professor Tyndall's words to the British Association meeting at Belfast in 1874: 'Two courses and two only are possible. Either let us open our doors freely to the conception of creative acts, or, abandoning them, let us radically change our notions of the Matter . . . The impregnable position of science may be described in a few words. We claim, and we shall wrest from theology, the entire domain of cosmological theory.' All but the most thoughtful or the most careless Christians tended to think there was a war on and they must take sides. Very few perceived the parallel nature of science and religion which is evident enough to most people nowadays.

We shall, alas, never know in any detail how it all appeared to Hardy for he gives no more account of the process of his loss of belief in the *Life* than he does of any other experiences that were traumatic or formative. The only writings that survive from the 1860s are a few poems such as 'Hap', which has already been mentioned, 'At a Bridal' (sub-titled 'Nature's Indifference'), '1967', 'In Vision I Roamed' and 'A Young Man's Epigram on Existence' which seem to express a bleakly pessimistic acceptance of the negative consequences of Darwinism. One is tempted to over-simplify the issue as a 'convergence of the twain' between the ardent, simple belief of the young Dorset man with the sceptical movements of his time. It is true that at no other moment in history could a belief so simple have collided with an iceberg so imposing. Possibly Hardy's inherited beliefs sank at once and he was left for the rest of his life surveying the waste of waters under which they had disappeared, dimly perceiving in their cold currents the outlines of the wreck and continually contemplating the possibilities of salvage. He ended *The Dynasts* nearly fifty years later with the vision of 'consciousness the Will informing/Till it fashion all things fair' which is straining rationalism very far and is little different from 'One far-off divine event,/To which the whole creation moves'; and in the many poems about religion, though never in the novels, which were written earlier, he expostulates again and again in every possible tone from the most tragic pleading to jocular banter with the lost anthropomorphic God – 'God as an external personality' – for his failure to exist and seems as often to be trying to coax him back into life as to bury him, as he does in 'God's Funeral'. He was a reluctant disbeliever and when at the end of that poem he *does* decide to follow the rest of humanity to the ceremonial interment of God and has found that he cannot associate himself with either the few who cling to the old religion or the small and prophetic band who look for the emergence of a new and truer one, he puts it in these words:

> Thus dazed and dazzled 'twixt the gleam and gloom,
> Mechanically, I followed with the rest.

But there must have been qualities in Hardy's belief and in his particular expectations of religion, as well as in the logical incompatibility between Christian belief and rationalistic science which all thinking people were forced to encounter, that caused him to sacrifice a thing he so much needed and valued, whose loss was so abiding and lifelong an emotional deprivation. I shall try and say something about what these may have been shortly. In any event, however painful a process loss of belief may have been, it did not make the 1860s a period only of suffering and doubt. Mrs Hardy writes in the *Life* that very soon before his death: 'While he was having tea today T. H. said that whenever he heard any music from *Il Trovatore*, it carried him back to the first year when he was in London and when he was strong and vigorous and enjoyed life immensely.' Further, the way in which he handled his loss of belief is biographically speaking a very odd one and suggests some peculiar mental processes underlying it. Unlike Leslie Stephen, who was a parson, Hardy had no need to secede from the church, but it *is* odd that the man who in 1866 had written those poems of doubt should eight years later, and presumably with his eyes wide open to what he was doing, have married into it. Everyone knows the story of the St Juliot idyll from *Poems of 1912–13* and from Emma Hardy's *Recollections* at the beginning of Chapter V of the *Life*. In 1870 Hardy became a frequent and welcome guest at the piously conventional rectory on the north coast of Cornwall, fell passionately in love with the rector's sister-in-law and after four years of close friendship she became his wife. Within a year of the marriage ceremony, which was of course celebrated in church, Hardy was disillusioned about the marriage and wrote in a poem called 'We Sat at The Window' (it was not published till 1917, five years after Emma's death, but describes a visit they paid to a Bournemouth boarding house in 1875):

> Waste were two souls in their prime,
> And great was the waste that July time
> When the rain came down.

Emma was a deeply committed Christian believer and emerges from the *Recollections* as a person with a good deal of intelligence and sensibility but with serious limitations and no desire whatever to reason about her belief. They were written in 1911, a year before she died, at Max Gate, that ugly house Hardy had himself designed for

her and where they were by then living on terms of near-estrange-
ment. But they present the same idealised view of the years 1870
to 1874 as do *Poems of 1912–13*. They begin by describing the zeal
and fervour of the rector – a 'very Boanerges in preaching' – and how
'after I went to live there with my sister-in-law, we were marshalled
off in regular style to the services', as the author of 'Hap' must have
been at weekends. Yet when Emma first met Hardy: 'I noticed a blue
paper sticking out of his pocket' which 'proved to be the MS. of a
poem, not a plan of the church, he informed me to my surprise . . .
When my Architect came to visit me, I rode my pretty mare Fanny
and he walked by my side'; and Hardy admired her physical beauty
and horsemanship. 'In the intervals of his visits, we corresponded . . .
After a time I copied a good deal of manuscript, which went to and
fro by post and I was very proud and happy doing so . . . The rarity
of the visits made them highly delightful to both; we talked much
of plots, possible scenes, tales and poetry and of his own work.' The
Recollections end:

The day we were married was a perfect September day . . . not of
brilliant sunshine but wearing a soft, sunny luminousness; just as
it should be. I have had various experiences, interesting some, sad
others, since that lovely day. But all showing that an Unseen Power
of great benevolence directs our ways; I have some philosophy,
and mysticism, and an ardent belief in Christianity and the life
beyond this present one, all which makes my existence curiously
interesting. As one watches happenings (and even if should occur
unhappy happenings), outward circumstances are of less importance
if Christ is our highest ideal. A strange unearthly brilliance shines
around our path penetrating and dispersing difficulties with its
warmth and glow.

It would be impossible to think of a fuller and more exact statement
of all that Hardy would have liked to believe and could not, of the
picture of human life and its meaning which his emotions so much
desired but were unable to sustain, than this account of herself by
his alienated and, as many believe, mentally deranged wife just
before the end of their thirty-eight years of marriage.

It seems inconceivable that the author of 'Hap' and the writer of
the *Recollections* could have felt and thought about each other
between 1870 and 74 as we are assured they did in Poems of 1912–13
(and as the *Recollections* confirm) if they had been aware of their
profound differences. Yet Robert Gittings[9] in his twelfth chapter
('Hardy and the Giffords') makes a good case for the fact that among
the manuscripts that Emma 'was very proud and happy' to copy for

her Architect, there must have been some of the early poems, parts at least of *The Poor Man and the Lady* (of which Alexander Macmillan wrote to Hardy : 'Thackeray means fun, but you mean mischief') and of the corrosively gloomy *Desperate Remedies* (whose hero at one point reflects that, as he puts it, human life is at best a brief episode between one darkness and another – that the normal human condition is to be dead). Could Emma have consented to marry Hardy if she had thought he really *believed* all that she found in these manuscripts? Could Hardy, with his deep honesty and rectitude of mind, have concealed the true nature of his thoughts, his decisive rejection of Christian belief from her? And, however many illusions both may have held about their relationship, could someone as psychologically acute and aware as Hardy have failed to foresee the unavoidable disaster inherent in a marriage between two people so little like-minded?

It is a mystery to which Hardy's many biographers have given too little attention. Lacking knowledge, one is driven back on conjecture, and my conjecture, supported by his lifelong and continual insistence that he never held any ideas, only impressions, that 'the views [in my works of art] are *seemings*, provisional impressions only, used for artistic purposes', is that Hardy must genuinely have persuaded both Emma and himself that this was true of the views she found in his manuscripts; that the Darwinian loss of belief recorded in the 1866 poems was far from the decisive rejection it appears to have been but a 'seeming' held in one part of his consciousness and not at all incompatible with his behaving as or seeming to be, and quite honestly in another part of his consciousness feeling that he was, the pious Anglican who was marshalled off to services by Mrs Holder and whom Emma married on that lovely day in 1874. I suggest further that it was the experience of living, after romance had given place to the reality of everyday life, with someone who held and practised Emma's beliefs, that united the two aspects of Hardy's mind and forced him for the first time to face the fact that his 'impressions' of the 1860s did amount to a total and decisive rejection; that Hardy's 'loss of belief' solidified in his mind for the first time in 1874–5. The convergence of the twain that had been adumbrated by his meeting with Darwinism and the Higher Criticism was a near miss, not a final wreck, and the real iceberg which sank Hardy's religion was Emma's belief. This, however conjectural, does at least account for the otherwise unaccountable fact of their embarking upon marriage with such high expectations and for the extraordinarily rapid disillusion and disappointment recorded in 'We Sat at The Window'.

Hardy celebrated his eighty-sixth birthday with a poem called 'He

Never Expected Much'. He liked in some moods to look upon his life as one of stoical resignation but

> When as a child I used to lie
> Upon the leaze and watch the sky
> Never, I own, expected I
> That life would be all fair.

is not an expression of modest expectations. Instinctively, anyhow, he expected a great deal more – he expected that life would all be fair. He had the temperament of a pre-lapsarian visionary and intuitively expected a harmonious universe animated by divine purpose and meaning, an immortal condition of peace and well-being for all creatures, and for man in particular the life of Eden, willed and sanctified by the paternal love of an immanent God – 'as an external personality, the only true meaning of the word' – with whom he would be on terms of absolute devotion and reverent personal intimacy, and consummated by a perfect and innocent sexual union in an existence free of death, sin or evil. It is of course a common archetype and is nowhere so well described as in *Paradise Lost*. It is useless to inquire why it should have survived at an unconscious level in Hardy's innermost feelings all through his life. One of his earliest recollections of childhood – 'he was lying on his back in the sun, thinking how useless he was, and covered his face with his straw hat. The sun's rays streamed through the interstices of the straw . . . he came to the conclusion that he did not wish to grow up . . . he did not want at all to be a man and possess things, but to remain as he was, in the same spot, and to know no more people than he already knew (about half a dozen)'[10] – is not so much, as Hardy interprets it, evidence of 'lack of social ambition' as a simple dream of unfading innocence. The paradisal vision is again and again discernible through the darkening mists of pessimistic rationalism. 'Before Life and After', written sixty years or more later, is ostensibly a 'meditation . . . upon the cruel accident of sentience'[11] but is really a passionate and positive evocation of a state of bliss where 'None suffered sickness, love, or loss,/None knew regret, starved hope, or heart-burnings'; and the paradoxical illogic that counts love among the fruits of the fall and makes human consciousness the snake that has perverted the garden – 'Ere nescience shall be reaffirmed/How long, how long?' – only emphasises the conflict between feeling and reason and intensifies the power of the poem. The subtlest and most sensitive of Hardy's interpreters, Benjamin Britten, has expressed its meaning perfectly in the song cycle *Winter Words* by setting the words not as a dirge but an idyll, and accompanying them on the piano by a simple, profound, majestic and miraculous realisation of the music of the spheres.

What gives all Hardy's mind and art their unique quality is that they do result from the disappointment and contradiction of this inalienably held vision of Paradise by the facts of experience in a fallen world. To the pre-lapsarian visionary, the inherently post-lapsarian qualities of mysticism and faith have no meaning. Adam didn't have to believe in God. He was quite evidently there. When it became apparent to Hardy that it was not as simple as that, he had, despite his intense emotional need of religious belief, no more sophisticated spiritual resources to fall back on and was forced to profess intellectually a pessimistic atheism quite unconnected with his interior vision. This is why, again and again, in the *Life* he seems to be evading the consequences of his rationalistic professions,[12] and never in fact declares himself either fully a believer or an unbeliever. 'The eternal question of what life was/And why we were there,'[13] which he read in the 'large, luminous living eyes' of Florence Dugdale, possessed him for ever but was never answered because the only answer that could have satisfied his feelings was the realisation of his vision of Eden.

The pre-lapsarian vision of sexual love is evident in all the poems of recollection of the St Juliot idyll. It is no derogation from the greatness of the poems to say that they are not about real people at all but about Adam and Eve in the garden – an allegory of perfect love, not fragments of autobiography – and that Florence Hardy was right when she wrote that their subject was 'a fiction but a fiction in which their author has now come to believe'.[14] The great novels are the most bleakly pessimistic tragedies ever written – far more hopeless than those of Sophocles, Shakespeare or Conrad for instance, who were not pre-lapsarian visionaries and who never knew unlimited expectations. Whatever Hardy may have professed or thought about himself, neither in the novels nor anywhere else does he 'see life steadily and see it whole', nor does he find a way to the better by taking a good look at the worst. He sees and articulates the difference between his interior vision of perfection and 'uncompromising rude reality'.[15] He finds no value in suffering, no attainment of self-knowledge through tragic experience. Neither Tess nor Jude gain any enlightenment as Oedipus does at Colonus, as Lear on the heath and the beach or as Axel Heyst on his island – they simply suffer and die meaninglessly in a hopeless universe. The derivation of the novels from the pre-lapsarian vision is emphasised by their frequent evocations of the idyllic – as in much of *The Woodlanders* or at Talbothays or, most significantly, in Tess's assurance to Abraham that the stars are 'like apples on our stubbard-tree. Most of them splendid and sound – a few blighted' and that we live on a blighted one, and by the pattern of invasion of their potential paradises by 'Mephistophelean visitants'. In *Jude* we seem to have reached the end of the road; nothing remains but despair, delusion, the final negation of hope. Yet even this proves to have been 'a *seeming*, a provisional impression used for artistic purposes'. Twelve years later Hardy ends *The Dynasts*, as he wrote, 'on a note of hope'[16] quite opposite to the conclusion of *Jude*. The poems about religion are likewise quite inconsistent. In some God is dead, in some he has never existed, in others he is very much alive and in a few he is even beneficent.[17] If we look to them or to anything Hardy wrote for the consistent exposition of a religion or an atheistic philosophy, we look for something that is not there. If we look to him for a dramatisation of the continually shifting, never resolved dialogue between his pre-lapsarian intuition and a conscious mind committed to frustrating it, we read aright.

Hardy was not a religious man in the sense in which Milton, T. S. Eliot or D. H. Lawrence were religious. He makes no attempt to harmonise or reconcile his intuition with his experience or to construct or proclaim a system or a faith. He is content to be 'a great seer and feeler'. But he cannot separate his religious impulse from the old traditional beliefs which depend more strongly upon the myth of Eden than on any sense that 'the Kingdom of God is within you'. When he wrote that 'Invidious critics [who] had cast slurs upon him as Nonconformist, Agnostic, Atheist, Infidel, Immoralist, Heretic, Pessimist, or something else equally opprobious in their eyes, had never thought of calling him what they might have called him much more plausibly – churchy; not in an intellectual sense, but insofar as instincts and emotions ruled,' he showed the profoundest self-knowledge – that wherever his reason may have led him in the intellectual circumstances of his time, his heart lay more deeply in the Church than in any original religious insight or genius.

As he lay dying, he reasserted 'my simple self that was' and in fact always persisted; he asked to hear some lines from the *Rubáiyát*:

> O, Thou, who Man of baser Earth didst make,
> And ev'n with Paradise devise the Snake:
> For all the sin wherewith the Face of Man
> Is blacken'd – Man's forgiveness give – and take!

To interpret this as has been done, as a deathbed recantation of rationalism is absurd. No lines could better express Hardy's lifelong predicament – his confusion between logically humanist and traditionally religious values nor could any better settle his account with a life which, at different times, in different moods, he saw as ruled by 'crass casualty', 'the President of the Immortals', The Will growing into consciousness, and even by a purposeful creator. In 'The Absolute Explains' and its coda 'So Time', written as late as 1922, Hardy returns to the idea of a divine plan and, at his most pre-lapsarian, to the abolition of time, change and death, and turns scientific rationalism to visionary purpose. In these poems the two extremes of his being meet in his understanding (or perhaps misunderstanding) of the theory of relativity and it was there that he found his final vision of Eden. In his diary for 10 June 1923 he wrote: 'Relativity. That things and events always were, are and will be (e.g. Emma, Mother and Father are still living in the past).'

NOTES

1 Jacques Monod, *Chance and Necessity* (London, 1972).
2 'A Plaint to Man'.
3 Monod, op. cit.
4 F. E. Hardy, *The Life of Thomas Hardy* (London, 1962) p. 332. I take it to be now generally accepted that this book, which originally appeared in two volumes in 1928 and 1930, is an autobiography in the third person and was written, except for the last chapter which Florence Hardy added after his death, by Hardy himself.
5 Ibid., p. 29.
6 Ibid., p. 224.
7 This was never better demonstrated than in the brilliant series of Gifford lectures on *Mind* given at the University of Edinburgh in the form of a dialogue between two eminent scientists and two equally eminent philosophers in 1971 and 1972. See A. J. P. Kenny and others, *The Nature of Mind* (Edinburgh, 1972) and *The Development of Mind* (Edinburgh, 1973).
8 David Lack, *Evolutionary Theory and Christian Belief* (London, 1957) p. 22.
9 Robert Gittings, *Young Thomas Hardy* (London, 1975).
10 *Life*, pp. 15–16. The words are, in their homely way, curiously reminiscent of Henry Vaughan's vision of 'those early days! when I/Shined in my angel-infancy/Before I understood this place/Appointed for my second race/Or taught my soul to fancy ought/But a white celestial thought'.
11 F. R. Leavis, *New Bearings in English Poetry*, London, 1967. Considering Hardy after fifty years, one is struck by the profound understanding of his dual nature shown by Britten in comparison with the outmoded judgements of earlier verbal critics, for example I. A. Richards for whom Hardy is 'the poet who has most steadfastly refused to be comforted . . . The comfort of forgetfulness, the comfort of beliefs, he has put both these away' (*Science and Poetry*, London, 1926): F. R. Leavis, for whom 'he industriously turns out his despondent anecdotes, his "life's little ironies" and his meditations on a deterministic universe and the cruel accident of sentience' (op. cit., p. 54, originally written in 1932); or Eliot, for whom '*The City of Dreadful Night*, and *A Shropshire Lad*, and the poems of Thomas Hardy are small work in comparison with *In Memoriam*; it is greater than they and comprehends them' (introduction to *Poems of Tennyson*, London, 1936).
12 A few among very many examples of this trait in the *Life* are Hardy's

remarks about church membership (pp. 332–3) and atheism (p. 376) and his refusal to allow his name to appear in a *Biographical Dictionary of Modern Rationalists* in 1920 (p. 403).

13 'After the Visit.'
14 W. Blunt. *Cockerell* (London, 1964, p. 223 n).
15 'God's Funeral.'
16 See *Life*, pp. 453–4. See also pp. 368 and 375–6 for Hardy's varying attitudes to the 'seemings' he uses as ideas.
17 He is *never* malignant or wilfully cruel, at worst unconscious or dimly uncomprehending. The President of the Immortals who ended his sport with Tess has been abandoned; and though a fitter epigraph for *Jude* than the Swinburnian one it bears might be '*Tantum religio potuit suadere malorum*', such a line as Housman's 'Whatever brute and blackguard made the world' is, even in the mouth of a *persona*, quite beyond the range of Hardy's reverence.

7 Thomas Hardy as a Cinematic Novelist

David Lodge

This essay is a revised and extended version of an article, 'Thomas Hardy and Cinematographic Form', published in *Novel*, VII (1974) pp. 246–54.

Thomas Hardy's last novel, *Jude the Obscure* (1895), was published well before film had properly evolved as a narrative medium. By calling him a 'cinematic' novelist, therefore, I mean that he anticipated film, not that he was influenced by it. In a general sense this is true of all the great nineteenth-century realistic novelists. As Leon Edel has observed:

> Novelists have sought almost from the first to become a camera. And not a static instrument but one possessing the movement through space and time which the motion-picture camera has achieved in our century. We follow Balzac, moving into his subject, from the city into the street, from the street into the house, and we tread hard on his heels as he takes us from room to room. We feel as if that massive 'realist' had a prevision of the cinema . . . Wherever we turn in the nineteenth century we can see novelists cultivating the camera-eye and the camera movement . . .[1]

One way of explaining this affinity between film and classic realistic fiction is to say that both are 'metonymic' forms, in Roman Jakobson's sense of that term. According to Jakobson, a discourse connects one topic with another either because they are *similar* to each other or because they are in some sense *contiguous* with each other in space-time. Most discourse uses both types of connection, but usually one or the other predominates. Jakobson calls them metaphoric and metonymic, respectively, because these tropes are models or epitomes of the processes involved: metaphor being a figure of substitution based on similarity, while metonymy (and the closely related figure of synecdoche) deletes from or rearranges naturally contiguous entities, substituting cause for effect or part for whole, or vice versa.

In Jakobson's scheme, drama and lyric poetry are typically metaphoric forms, while film and realistic prose fiction are typically metonymic. 'Following the path of contiguous relationships, the realistic author metonymically digresses from the plot to the atmosphere and from the characters to the setting in space and time', says Jakobson (this matches Edel's description of Balzac's technique exactly). 'He is fond of synecdochic detail. In the scene of Anna Karenina's suicide Tolstoy's attention is focused on the heroine's handbag . . .'[2] The handbag is a synecdoche for Anna. It will be remembered that she throws it aside as she jumps beneath the train, and that her first attempt is checked when the bag becomes entangled in her clothing. One could easily imagine a cinematic treatment of the scene in which the camera cuts away from the fatal leap to a close-up shot of the poignantly abandoned handbag on the platform. Close-up is the filmic equivalent of synecdoche (part standing for whole). Film has its metaphors too, of course (e.g. waves pounding on the shore signifying sexual intercourse in the pre-permissive cinema), but this kind of montage must be used sparingly in narrative film, or disguised as contextual detail, if intelligibility is to be preserved. For the same reasons modernist or symbolist novels in which the metaphorical principle of similarity largely determines the development of the discourse (e.g. Joyce's *Ulysses*) are much more difficult to translate into film than realistic novels.

'Realism' as an aesthetic effect depends upon the suppression of overt reference to the conventions employed, so that the discourse seems to be a transparent window on reality, rather than a code. Avant-garde and experimental movies may draw attention to their own optics, but most narrative films do not. As experienced viewers of films we tend to take the camera eye for granted and to accept the truthfulness of what it shows us. Though its perspective is never that of ordinary human vision, it is close enough to the latter to seem a transparent medium for the rendering of reality rather than an artificial system of signs. Similarly the narrative style of realistic fiction, derived from non-fictional types of discourse such as biography, confession, letters and historiography, bestows upon the fictitious narrative a pseudo-historical authenticity. Both novel and film are able to shift their point of view between an 'omniscient' or impersonal perspective and the perspective of a particular character without sacrificing realistic illusion. Roland Barthes has observed that 'the discourse of the traditional novel alternates the personal and the impersonal very rapidly, often in the same sentence, so as to produce, if we can speak thus, a proprietary consciousness which retains the

mastery of what it states without participating in it',[3] and the same
may be said of film.

If there is so close an affinity between the classic realistic novel
and film, what is the justification for distinguishing Hardy as a
'cinematic novelist'? To answer that question we must emphasise
the *differences* between novel and film. Apart from dialogue and
monologue (which are available to both) and the use of music for
emotive suggestion, film is obliged to tell its story purely in terms of
the visible – behaviour, physical appearance, setting – whereas the
verbal medium of the novel can describe anything, visible or invisible
(notably the thoughts passing through a character's head), and can do
so as abstractly as it pleases. A cinematic novelist, then, is one who, as
it were, deliberately renounces some of the freedom of representation
and report afforded by the verbal medium, who imagines and presents
his materials in primarily visual terms, and whose visualisations
correspond in some significant respect to the visual effects characteristic of film.

That description, especially description of the natural settings of his
stories, plays a crucially important part in Thomas Hardy's fiction
is, of course, a commonplace. But I don't think it has been observed
how remarkably 'cinematic' he is, both in the way he describes landscape and in the way he deploys his human figures against it. Hardy
uses verbal description as a film director uses the lens of his camera
– to select, highlight, distort and enhance, creating a visualised
world that is both recognisably 'real' and yet more vivid, intense and
dramatically charged than our ordinary perception of the real world.
The methods he uses can be readily analysed in cinematic terms:
long shot, close-up, wide-angle, telephoto, zoom, etc. Indeed, some of
Hardy's most original visual effects have since become cinematic
clichés. One thinks of his use of mirrors to dramatise encounters in
which there is an element of guilt, suspense or deception (e.g.
Eustacia realising that Clym had discovered the truth about her
treatment of his mother when she sees his grim face reflected in the
mirror of her dressing-table, or Grace in *The Woodlanders* startled
to discover in the mirror of Fitzpiers' sitting-room that he is regarding
her from his couch, though when she turns round he is apparently
asleep);[4] and his use of 'aerial shots' (of Tess on the floor of the valley
of the Great Dairies, for instance, or of Wildeve and Eustacia on
Egdon Heath at night in *The Return of the Native*).[5]

Hardy, like a film-maker, seemed to conceive his fictions, from the
beginning, as human actions in a particular setting: the dense woods
of *The Woodlanders*, the wild heathland of *The Return of the Native*,
the contrasting valleys and heights of *Tess*, are integral to the

imaginative unity of those novels. He called them 'novels of character and environment', and it is his ability to make concrete the
relationship between character and environment in a way that is
both sensuously particular and symbolically suggestive that makes
him such a powerful and original novelist, in my opinion, rather than
his skill in story-telling, his insight into human motivation or his
philosophic wisdom. This emphasis on the visual presentation of experience makes him no less of a *writer* – quite the contrary, since he
must do through language what the film-maker can do by moving
his camera and adjusting his lens; correspondingly, it is difficult for
film adaptation to do justice to Hardy's novels precisely because
effects that are unusual in written description are commonplace in
film.[6]

To illustrate my argument I will comment in some detail on the
opening chapters of *The Return of the Native* (1878). This novel
begins, like so many films, with an emotionally loaded, panoramic
establishing shot of the *mise-en-scène*, Egdon Heath:

> A Saturday afternoon in November was approaching the time of
> twilight, and the vast tract of unenclosed wild known as Egdon
> Heath embrowned itself moment by moment. Overhead the hollow
> stretch of whitish cloud shutting out the sky was as a tent which
> had the whole heath for its floor.

The emphasis in the first chapter is on the heath's symbolic proper-
ties, especially its consonance with the mood of late nineteenth-century cosmic pessimism in which this novel is, a little self-indulgently,
steeped. For this purpose the heath is empty (Chapter 2 is headed,
'Humanity appears upon the Scene, Hand in Hand with Trouble')
but it is noteworthy that at several points Hardy postulates an
observer as a kind of descriptive formula: 'Looking upwards, a furze-
cutter would have been inclined to continue work; looking down, he
would have decided to finish his faggot and go home' . . . 'To recline
on a stump of thorn in the central valley of Egdon, between afternoon and night, as now, where the eye could reach nothing of the
world outside the summits and shoulders of heathland which filled
the whole circumference of its glance' . . . 'On the evening under
consideration it would have been noted that, though the gloom had
increased sufficiently to confuse the minor features of the heath, the
white surface of the road remained almost as clear as ever.'

The invocation of a hypothetical or unspecified observer in description is one of the signatures of Hardy's narrative style. His novels
are full of phrases like, 'An observer would have remarked', 'a
loiterer in this place might have speculated', or verbs of perception,

often in the passive voice ('it was seen', 'it was felt', etc.) that are not attached to any specified subect. Why should a novelist who did not shrink from exercising the authorial privilege of intrusive philosophical comment feel compelled to invent surrogates for himself when it came to description? The habit is linked with Hardy's heavy reliance on *specified* observers in his fiction: there are an extraordinary number of scenes in which one character observes, spies on or eavesdrops on others. J. Hillis Miller has plausibly traced this feature of Hardy's novels to the writer's own unconscious wish 'to escape from the dangers of direct involvement in life and to imagine himself in a position where he could safely see life as it is without being seen and could report on that seeing'.[7] But we may also interpret Hardy's reliance on specified and unspecified observers as evidence of the importance he attached to visual perspective – it is as though he is trying to naturalise devices of presentation that would require no such explanation or justification in film. These observing eyes act like camera lenses – and if there is often something voyeuristic about their observations, this only reminds us that film is a deeply voyeuristic medium.

To return to the *Native*: the opening paragraph of Chapter 2 introduces an old man, walking along the road whose whiteness was remarked at the close of Chapter 1. The physical appearance of the old man is described, followed by these words: 'One would have said that he had been, in his day, a naval officer of some sort or other.' Again, the unspecified observer: 'One would have said . . .' There is nothing to prevent Hardy from telling us that this is Captain Vye, retired, but he prefers to enact the process by which we interpret purely visual information, thus restricting himself voluntarily to a limitation that is binding on the film-maker. The old man now becomes the 'lens' through which we see. The road stretches before him, 'dry, empty and white. It was quite open to the heath on each side, and bisected that vast dark surface like a parting line on a head of black hair, diminishing and bending away on the furthest horizon.' Then, 'at length he discerned, a long distance in front of him, a moving spot which appeared to be a vehicle . . . It was the single atom of life that the scene contained.' This is a very characteristic, and very cinematic, effect in Hardy's fiction: the little speck of human life in a vast expanse of nature, expressing (though one doesn't wish to interpret too allegorically) the vulnerability of the individual human life, its relative insignificance in the temporal and spatial scale of the earth and the universe at large.

Gradually Captain Vye overtakes the van, which turns out to be 'ordinary in shape, but singular in colour, this being a lurid red. The driver walked beside it; and like his van, he was completely red.'

In a Technicolor film, this would surely be a stunning moment. Indeed, Diggory Venn the reddleman is one of Hardy's most cinematically-conceived characters. There is little to him psychologically: he is honest, chivalrous, loyal, a rather dull 'goodie'. The interest and appeal of his character is all in his picturesque appearance and behaviour: his weird pigmentation, his lonely nomadic existence, his dramatic interventions into the action – notably the scene in Chapter 8 of Part III where, like the strong silent hero of a Western, he strides into the circle of lamplight on the heath where Christian has just lost to Wildeve all the money entrusted to him by Mrs Yeobright:

> Wildeve stared. Venn looked coolly towards Wildeve, and without a word being spoken, he deliberately sat himself down where Christian had been seated, thrust his hand into his pocket, drew out a sovereign, and laid it on the stone.
>
> 'You have been watching us from behind that bush?' said Wildeve.
>
> The reddleman nodded. 'Down with your stake,' he said. 'Or haven't you pluck enough to go on?'

In Chapter 2 of Part I, Diggory, having been presented to us first through the eyes of Captain Vye, himself provides the eyes through which we first glimpse the heroine of the story, Eustacia Vye: a carefully composed visual sequence that begins with a wide-angle shot of the heath and then zooms in on the distant barrow where a figure is outlined against the sky.

> There the form stood, motionless as the hill beneath. Above the plain rose the hill, above the hill rose the barrow, and above the barrow rose the figure. Above the figure was nothing that could be mapped elsewhere than on a celestial globe . . . The figure perceptibly gave up its fixity, shifted a step or two, and turned round. As if alarmed, it descended on the right side of the barrow, with the glide of a water drop down a bud, and then vanished. The movement had been sufficient to show more clearly the characteristics of the figure, and that it was a woman's.
>
> The reason of her sudden displacement now appeared. With her dropping out of sight on the right side, a newcomer, bearing a burden, protruded into the sky on the left side, ascended the tumulus, and deposited the burden on the top. A second followed, then a third, a fourth, a fifth, and ultimately the whole barrow was peopled with burdened figures.
>
> The only intelligible meaning in this sky-backed pantomime

D

of silhouettes was that the woman had no relation to the forms who had taken her place, was sedulously avoiding these, and had come thither for another object than theirs.

Once again information is conveyed to the reader through visualised action, made striking and vivid by an unusual perspective, interpreted by a narrator who could have used his authorial privilege to simply *tell* us the facts.

The third chapter begins characteristically: 'Had a looker-on been posted in the immediate vicinity of the barrow, he would have learned that these persons were boys and men of the neighbouring hamlets.' The transition from Diggory's distant view-point to the hypothetical 'looker-on' is equivalent to a cinematic 'cut' from a long-distance shot to a close-up of a given subject. It situates us on the barrow, able to observe the local rustics as they build their bonfire, and to overhear their conversation. And now *they* become the observing eyes of the narrative, surveying the dark expanse of Egdon on which 'Red suns and tufts of fire one by one began to arise, flecking the whole country round. They were the bonfires of other parishes . . .'

To work through the entire novel in this way would be tedious, and I hope I have indicated clearly enough my grounds for regarding *The Return of the Native* as a 'cinematic novel' *avant la lettre*. That it is the product of an intensely *visual* imagination is surely undeniable. The plot, *qua* plot – considered as a sequence of human actions connected by cause and effect – has little to recommend it, heavily dependent as it is on melodramatic stereotypes in character and action. Yet we scarcely register these things as flaws because they are overlaid by, or are actually the occasion of, stunning visual effects. The reasons, the circumstances, that cause Eustacia not to open the cottage door to her mother-in-law, thus bringing about the latter's death and eventually her own, matter less than the visual image, perceived by Mrs Yeobright and frequently recalled later, of Eustacia's cold, hostile face at the window. The business of the gold guineas which are won by Wildeve from Christian, and then by Diggory from Wildeve, is not particularly interesting as plot, is indeed, entirely dispensable on this level, but one would be sorry to lose that memorable and intensely visual scene where the two men gamble on desperately into the night, surrounded by insects and cattle attracted by the light, and then, their candle extinguished by a moth, continue their game by the light of glow-worms. The same is true of the characters. For instance, all Hardy's efforts to dignify Eustacia with classical allusion cannot make her into a complex or morally interesting character. She is essentially a rather shallow-minded, self-dramatising young woman, primarily interesting (like many heroines of the screen) because of her physical beauty, which Hardy evokes very powerfully by close-ups of her lips, throat, eyes and hair ('rich romantic lips' and 'beautiful stormy eyes' are representative phrases), and by posing her picturesquely against the background of the heath.

Subtract all description of the heath from the novel, and you would be left with a rather contrived melodrama of unhappy love, relieved by some amusing comic dialogue from the rustics. The novel as we have it, with the descriptions of Egdon, is powerful and memorable. A line in Chapter 7 of Book Four, 'moving figures began to animate the line between heath and sky', epitomises the characteristic visual motif of the novel, established in its opening chapters: the two masses of heath and sky, one dark and the other lighter, both inscrutable and indifferent to the pathetically small, vulnerable human figures occasionally visible against these backgrounds. Usually the perspective is horizontal, but on at least one occasion Hardy switches to the vertical, when Wildeve and Eustacia are walking back from the country dance:

> The moon had now waxed bright and silvery, but the heath was proof against such illumination, and there was to be observed the striking scene of a dark, rayless tract of country under an atmosphere charged from its zenith to its extremities with whitest light. To an eye above them their two faces would have appeared amid the expanse like two pearls on a table of ebony. (IV, 3)

This emphasis throughout the novel on the smallness and vulnerability of the human being is conveyed primarily through panoramic views with deep perspective, combined with effects of 'zooming in' on distant figures. But it is worth noting that Hardy's visual imagination is just as active in close-up treatment of small-scale subjects. As blindness encroaches on Clym, for example,

> His daily life was of a curious microscopic sort, his whole world being limited to a circuit of a few feet from his person. His familiars were creeping and winged things . . . Bees hummed around his ears with an intimate air, and tugged at the heath and furze-flowers at his side in such numbers as to weigh them down to the sod. The strange amber-coloured butterflies which Egdon produced, and which were never seen elsewhere, quivered in the breath of his lips, alighted upon his bowed back, and sported with the glittering point of his hook as he flourished it up and down. Tribes of emerald-green grasshoppers leaped over his feet, falling awk-

wardly on their backs, heads or hips, like unskilful acrobats . . .
Litters of young rabbits came out from their forms to sun themselves upon hillocks, the hot beams blazing through the delicate
tissue of each thin-fleshed ear, and firing it to a blood-red trans-
parency in which the veins could be seen. (IV, 2)

This passage has the eye-opening beauty of a good natural history
film, and in the treatment of the grasshoppers anticipates the witty
anthropomorphism of Disney at his best.

Hardy's most powerful and characteristic descriptive passages are
generally 'exteriors'; but it is worth noting that his treatment of
interiors is equally cinematic, both in the way he lights them and
in his choice of viewpoints from which to observe them. *The Woodlanders* is especially rich in instances of this kind, perhaps because
the dense, all-enclosing woods in which the action is mainly set made
impossible the broad, panoramic descriptions of scenery at which
Hardy excelled. (The notable exception is that remarkable scene in
Chapter 28, so like a film Western in effect, when Grace watches
Fitzpiers cross White Hart Vale on her horse Darling, the setting sun
catching the white coat of the horse and making it visible until it is
a mere speck on the opposite ridge.) In Chapter 2, Barber Percomb
regards the unsuspecting Marty South through the open door of her
cottage as she sits making spars by the light of her fire, which is also
dimly and ominously reflected in the scissors protruding from the
barber's waistcoat pocket. Here, as so often, Hardy invokes the art
of painting to convey the particular visual effect he had in mind, but
it is one that the cinema has since made very familiar:

In her present beholder's mind the scene formed by the girlish
spar-maker composed itself into an impression-picture of extremest
type, wherein the girl's hair alone, as the focus of observation,
was depicted with intensity and distinctness, while her face,
shoulders, hands, and figure in general were a blurred mass of
unimportant detail lost in haze and obscurity.

The situation in which a figure in an illuminated interior is observed
from outside, through a door or window, is a recurrent motif in the
novel. After bringing Grace back to her home in Chapter 6, Giles,
outside the house, wistfully watches through a door the family
gathered round the parlour fire, and observes an effect of light on
Grace's hair similar to that described in the earlier scene. Immediately
afterwards Grace is alerted to the presence of Fitzpiers in the wood-
land by the coloured lights in his window. Later, Giles sees Grace
looking at herself in her bedroom mirror by candlelight as she

anticipates the next day's visit to Mrs Charmond (Chapter 7). When Giles agrees to keep Fitzpiers company on his nocturnal drive in Chapter 16, the latter identifies Grace when they both catch sight of her drawing the curtains of her bedroom. After summoning Fitzpiers to attend Mrs Charmond following her accident, Giles 'stepped back into the darkness . . . and . . . stood for a few minutes looking at the window which, by its light, revealed the room where Grace was sitting' (Chapter 26). When Fitzpiers is asked to leave the Melbury house, he does so without meeting her, but 'while passing through the gate he turned his head. The firelight of the room she sat in threw her figure into dark relief against the window as she looked through the panes, and he must have seen her distinctly' (Chapter 44). The most bizarre variation on this theme, with the point of observation reversed, comes in Chapter 36 when Mrs Charmond pulls back the shutter of her drawing-room window to reveal on the other side of the pane, 'the face of Fitzpiers . . . surrounded with the darkness of the night without, corpse-like in its pallor, and covered with blood' – a moment worthy of Hitchcock.

Hardy's most stunning visual effects are however never introduced just 'for effect' (as they are sometimes in Hitchcock); they are invariably part of some larger aesthetic and thematic pattern. The recurrent motif in *The Woodlanders* of the illuminated figure inside, observed by an unobserved observer outside, symbolises the imperfect understanding and defective communication that obtains between the main characters in the novel; just as the diminutive figures on the rim of a huge horizontal landscape in *The Return of the Native* symbolise the vulnerability of human creatures and the indifference of Nature to their agonies and ecstasies. The same kind of patterning of visual effect is observable in the most substantial relic we have of Hardy's first work of fiction, *The Poor Man and the Lady*. Before Hardy destroyed the manuscript of this work, he carved out of it a short serial story, called 'An Indiscretion in the Life of an Heiress', which was published in the *New Quarterly Magazine* in 1878, and recently reprinted in book form.[8] The plot is simple and melodramatic: Egbert Mayne, a gifted but poor young man, falls imprudently in love with Geraldine, the beautiful daughter of the local squire, and she with him. He goes to London to make his fortune, and after a number of years have passed she almost gives herself in loveless marriage to an aristocratic suitor. After a dramatic meeting on the eve of the wedding the lovers elope and marry. The strain of attempting a reconciliation with her stern father, however, proves fatal to Geraldine. The story is certainly among Hardy's less impressive achievements, as he acknowledged by excluding it from his collected works, but it demonstrates his ability to give power and poignancy to commonplace and even stereotyped emotions by artful effects of lighting and perspective. The opening chapter, set in a parish church closely modelled on Hardy's own at Stinsford, is representative in this respect. Afternoon service in winter is in progress. From the gallery Egbert looks down intently at Geraldine in her pew below, as the natural light fades from the windows:

The lady was the single person besides the preacher whose face was turned westwards, the pew that she occupied being the only one in the church in which the seat ran all around. She reclined in her corner, her bonnet and dress growing by degrees invisible, and at last only her upturned face could be discerned, a solitary white spot against the black surface of the wainscot. Over her head rose a vast marble monument, erected to the memory of her ancestors, male and female; for she was of high standing in that parish. The design consisted of a winged skull and two cherubim, supporting a pair of tall Corinthian columns, between which spread a broad slab, containing the roll of ancient names, lineages, and deeds, and surmounted by a pediment, with the crest of the family at its apex.

As the youthful schoolmaster gazed, and all these details became dimmer, her face was modified in his fancy, till it seemed almost to resemble the carved marble skull immediately above her head.[9]

This intensely visualised scene symbolises the social gap between the lovers, expresses the effort of will required of Egbert to maintain their relationship, and hints at its tragic conclusion. All the most important encounters between the lovers take place in darkness, or the melancholy half-darkness that follows dusk or precedes dawn, fitfully illuminated by candlelight or firelight: their first embrace, their parting when Egbert leaves for London, their meeting on the eve of the wedding. The final fatal meeting of Geraldine with her father also takes place at night, and its melodramatic character is somewhat muted by the fact that it is not presented directly. Instead, as Geraldine goes into the house, the narrative stays outside in the dark grounds with the anxious Egbert. The passage subtly echoes the opening scene in the church:

he watched her crossing the grass and advancing, a mere dot, towards the mansion. In a short time the appearance of an oblong of light in the shadowy expanse of wall denoted to him that the door was open: her outline appeared on it; then the door shut her in, and all was shadow as before. (Chapter 7)

Nothing could be more 'cinematic' – the best word, it seems to me, to describe what Hardy himself called his 'idiosyncratic mode of regard'.[10]

NOTES

1 Leon Edel, 'Novel and Camera', *The Theory of the Novel*, ed. John Halperin (New York, 1974) p. 177.
2 Roman Jakobson, 'Two Aspects of Language and Two Types of Linguistic Disturbances' in R. Jakobson and M. Halle, *Fundamentals of Language* (The Hague, 1956) p. 78. For a full discussion of the theory see my *The Modes of Modern Writing: Metaphor, Metonymy and the Typology of Modern Literature* (1977).
3 Roland Barthes, 'To Write: An Intransitive Verb?', *The Structuralist Controversy*, ed. R. Macksey and E. Donato (Baltimore, 1972) p. 140.
4 *The Return of the Native* v, 3; *The Woodlanders*, Chapter 18.
5 *Tess of the d'Urbervilles*, Chapter 16; *The Return of the Native*, iv, 3.
6 John Schlesinger's *Far from the Madding Crowd* (1967) made a good attempt in the early part of the film – particularly with a striking shot in which the camera moves rapidly and vertically away from Gabriel's flock until the sheep and the contours of the countryside become two-dimensional shapes in an abstract design – but gradually the melodrama of the story came to predominate.
7 J. Hillis Miller, *Thomas Hardy: Distance and Desire* (1970) p. 43.
8 Thomas Hardy, *An Indiscretion in the Life of an Heiress*, ed. with an introduction by Terry Coleman (1976).
9 This passage adapts a similar moment of speechless courtship in Stinsford church between Hardy's own parents, which he made the subject of a poem, 'A Church Romance: (Mellstock *circa* 1835)'.
10 In *The Life of Thomas Hardy* (London, 1962) p. 225.

8 Lawrence on Hardy

Mark Kinkead-Weekes

Perhaps the most brilliant and certainly the most individual essay on Hardy has been sadly neglected. Although D. H. Lawrence's *Study of Thomas Hardy* was written in 1914, it was only published in 1936, among the large miscellany of essays and sketches gathered in *Phoenix*.[1] Too long and complex to be included in collections of essays on Hardy, too short to be published alone, the *Study* has led a fugitive existence in Hardy criticism, more referred to than read, and certainly more read in anthologised extracts torn from context than as a coherent whole. Recently, it is true, the *Study* has become a recognised stopping-place for critics of Lawrence en route for *The Rainbow* and seeking some help with the 'ideas' which inform that novel. Yet extrapolation of 'ideas' has done little justice either to the imaginative quality of the work, or to the impact of Hardy at this crucial moment of Lawrence's development. As a book, supporting the claims of its title, it remains virtually ignored. There are however reasons for this. The bulk of the *Study* appears to be concerned with Lawrence, seemingly at his most arcane. It is also a study of art and the artist in painting as well as literature; a book about sex and marriage and not having enough to live on in 1914; a response to the outbreak of war. In a 'miserable world' it is a confession of faith[2] about creativity in nature, human relationship and art; a 'philosophy' or even 'theology' by a 'passionately religious man'[3] trying to adapt the language of Christianity to express his growing insight into the relation of man and woman. It is an attempt to clarify what he had been struggling towards in a novel he had thought was complete, but which had to be taken up again and restructured, with a newly sharp sense of form and purpose, as soon as the *Study* was finished. In all this, it is not too surprising that the sections actually on Hardy should seem isolated and disjunct. Yet the sense in which the book is any of these things is also the sense in which it is all, and Hardy is the centre. What I would like to indicate, within the limits of a short essay, is a way of reading which could make the *Study* more available not simply to the student of Lawrence's development, but to the student of the Wessex novels.

Inescapably, the account will seem to be more 'of Lawrence' than 'of Hardy'; but this is to overlook the mode of the book, which has more in common with creative than with critical writing. It is an imaginative exploration, beginning in one position, moving out into another, and concluding in a third; and in that exploration, though Lawrence is the traveller, it is Hardy who defines the journey. Though Hardy appears, so to speak, only on three separate occasions, each appearance is a dramatic intervention marking a phase of exploration, and summoning Lawrence to a more radical self-scrutiny. Seen like this, Hardy is not there for Lawrence as merely a text for a literary critic, but as a profoundly creative influence, shaping his own imagination in an unfolding drama whose resolution – in one's response – ought to be a final recognition of the nature of both protagonists.

Lawrence begins, however, not with Hardy, but with a poppy – and it is important to see why. We might start by disinguishing his kind of thinking from Eliot's, in opening *Notes towards the Definition of Culture*. ('The term *culture* has different associations according to whether we have in mind the development of an *individual*, of a *group* or *class*, or of a *whole society* . . .'[4]) Lawrence is to be no less concerned with culture (the tending of natural growth), the individual, and society; but he is not concerned with the kind of thinking that puts reason to work on terms, definitions, concepts. Human growth, in life or art, is an aspect of life itself, so Lawrence seeks to capture at the start a sense of something alive. This involves a consonant liveliness : a tone which refuses to take Lawrence or 'Man' too solemnly; a teasing humour which loosens up attitudes; an energy and fun which allow writer and reader to be on holiday with once-upon-a-time stories of cavemen, and phoenixes, and pastry-knobs on pies, and Dido. (One still comes across people who solemnly aver that Lawrence lacks humour.) But behind this is a grasp of parable as a way of getting down to basics, of teasing the intellectual scribe or pharisee out of conceptual thought into the extraordinary challenge of simplicity. Lawrence is, after all, obeying the charge to consider the lilies of the field, how they grow; and enforcing the same challenge as Christ's, to take no thought of self-preservation. To consider a poppy, growing, alive, is to see deeper and more simply than its 'careful architecture, all the chemistry, the weaving and the casting of energy' (399); it is to treat with contempt the concept of the red flower as the excess which always accompanies reproduction, or as a mere device to bring bees and help propagation. It is its flowering that makes a poppy a poppy : the thing itself at its maximum being.

As against, then, the urge to self-preservation from which society,

government and industry have evolved, Lawrence contends that the
final aim of every living thing is the full achievement of itself – after
which it will bear the fruit of its nature. In the second chapter he
reads this back into a radical criticism of society. If society is sick
in its political, sexual and economic relationships, if there is war, the
cause lies within individual men and women and there is no remedy
in seeking to reform social systems. The suffragettes (whom he respects), and movements for parliamentary, legal and economic reform,
are all misdirected towards the symptoms rather than the disease.
That lies in the urge to self-preservation itself, the obsession with
material needs, and the fear of risking security in the only final
human right: to be oneself to the maximum of one's individual
nature. For this very little is materially necessary (as Christ thought
too); but men fear it as they fear the unknown. Yet for Lawrence, as
for Blake, to repress the inner drive to be oneself, is inevitably to
produce rottenness and destruction. Even the pity which seeks to
redress poverty, 'loving one's neighbour as oneself', is false and
destructive if it means reducing one's sense of one's neighbour or
oneself to a matter of material needs; or if it leads to the false
egalitarianism of holding back the self-development of any so that
none should grow further than his neighbour. 'Every step I move
forward into being brings a newer, juster proportion into the world,
gives me less need of storehouse and barn, allows me to leave all,
and to take what I want by the way, sure that it will always be
there; allows me in the end to fly the flag of myself, at the extreme
tip of life' (409) – like a poppy, or a phoenix, or a kindled bonfire on
the edge of space. (The outbreak of war, on the other hand, is a sign
of the loss of all sense of the value of life, a mass-movement of self-
hate, a reaction of nausea against self-preservation, a death-wish.)

It is defiantly, even outrageously said, with a Blakean kind of truth,
though it will hardly do as it stands. At least, however, Lawrence
was practising what he preached. It is useful to realise that this
chapter was primarily addressed to himself and his own cry 'What is
going to become of us?'[5] when Methuen's return of his novel meant
that there was not going to be enough to live on. Only now does he
turn to Hardy, and only now can one see why the first of the three
essays on the Wessex novels should take the line it does – and why
it should be *The Return of the Native* that occupies the centre.
Humour returns in a cheerfully cavalier précis of the first six novels
as variations on a single theme – vastly oversimplified, of course. Yet
the X-ray picture of the walled city, the poppy-characters, and the
wilderness does have disconcerting insight, especially in the remarkable diagnosis of *The Return of the Native* which is Lawrence's real
concern. There are three main contentions. The typical Hardy

tragedy comes from the attempt to fulfil the self by breaking the confines of established forms of life in the community and its social morality; but the poppy-characters perish in the wilderness or come back reduced, while the prize of happiness and stability goes to those who stay within the walls. So the tragedy in *The Return* is the waste of Eustacia, through the 'subtle cowardice' and ultimate conventionality of Clym, who has original force of life but chooses 'to improve mankind rather than to struggle at the quick of himself into being' (414), and is consequently reduced to half-blindness and half-life, while Thomasin and Venn get the prize within the walls. But the second contention, which Lawrence urges more cogently than any other critic, is that Egdon Heath is the great power in the book. 'This is a constant revelation in Hardy's novels: that there exists a great background, vital and vivid, which matters more than the people who move upon it . . . The vast, unexplored morality of life itself, what we call the immorality of nature, surrounds us in its eternal incomprehensibility, and in its midst goes on the little human morality play' (419). Hardy shares this quality with the great writers, Shakespeare, Sophocles, Tolstoy. But, finally, Hardy and Tolstoy are smaller because their tragedy lies not in transgression of nature, but merely of society, which for Lawrence is not necessarily tragic at all.

Of course this is Lawrence's *Return of the Native* rather than Hardy's. This first criticism is too skeletal: the bone structure without the play of expression across the face. It ignores the many-sidedness of Hardy's vision and the curiously shifting relation between the author and the fiction. It produces an Eustacia too tragically heightened and released from ironies, a reddleman too reduced from enigmatic suggestiveness, an Egdon too much a Lawrentian life-force to be faithful to Hardy's multiple view of the heath and its inhabitants. Yet the deep structure Lawrence sees is there, significantly so; and the analysis of Clym is in many respects sharper than Hardy's own Victorian uncertainty about his hero. What is most significant, however, and seldom grasped, is that this first essay on Hardy is only an initial move. Lawrence is about to change his mind, and the direction of his exploration.

His fourth chapter, 'An Attack on Work, and the Money Appetite, and the State', is apparently an extension of the earlier argument. Potentially man is a constantly brimming fountain of life, but he mostly has to spend it in work. It is true that he must work to eat, but he must not merely eat to work again; he needs the means of self-preservation not just to exist, but to live more fully. There is a satisfaction in work, in executing efficiently an habitual movement or a known process; the happiness and security of staying 'safe within the proven, deposited experience' of humanity, as it were within 'the trunk of the tree, in the channels long since built' (424). But this is always, in the end, an imprisonment; for man's deepest urge is to project himself as a leading-shoot into further realms of being, and so he will always long to be free from work, 'for the unresolved, quivering, infinitely complex and indefinite movement of new living' (425). He must claim this freedom. The machine is a labour-saver which can help us produce all we really need, and can be honoured thus far; but it is time for man to renounce his greed for more than he needs, to renounce the money appetite which governs industrialist and worker alike, to affirm that the individual is more important than the state, to move outside the walled city of the existing system.

Yet something new is happening, suggested perhaps by the meta-phor of the tree, for in the next chapter Lawrence has changed his mind about work. It is not, after all, mere self-preservation but something more creative: a kind of knowledge, as man learned to plough and sow by becoming conscious of the significance of the fall of seeds and the covering of earth. So man is dual, Janus-faced: in both being ('the living stuff of life itself, unrevealed'); and 'knowing, with unwearying labour and unceasing success, the manner of that which has been, which is revealed' (430). Knowledge is also a force of life: 'It seems as if the great aim and purpose in human life were to bring all life into the human consciousness' (430–1); and as if conscious knowledge, involving increasing self-distinction of the individual from that which is not-him, were part of a universal process of progressive differentiation, from mass, to orders, to species, to distinct individual, to perfected individual, hero, or angel. Still the movement into being is primary, for knowledge can only be of that which already is; but the new sense of the value of distinct individuality forces Lawrence, in the middle of his chapter, to go back to Hardy again, from a different point of view.

The 'great background' is in abeyance, and the focus is now on the characters. Lawrence still urges his previous argument, but sees more clearly now that Hardy, too, has a *prédilection d'artiste* for the 'aristocrat' – by which he means someone who believes he or she has a right 'to be himself, to create himself' (436), to 'fulfil his own individual nature' (439) – as against the 'bourgeois', meaning some-one whose existence and loyalty are tied to the community. But this makes it all the more striking that all the aristocrats are doomed to failure or death, and that it is the bourgeois who prosper. The physical aristocrats fall before the community; the physical and spiritual aristocrats fall because of their own isolation; the physical aristocrats who are spiritually bourgeois fail physically and are reabsorbed into the community; the bourgeois with civic virtues usually succeeds in the end. But there are three new kinds of perception. If Hardy, having a predilection for the aristocrats, is so driven to show them destroyed by the community or create them fatally flawed, it must be because of some deep division in himself. Moreover, to follow the 'little morality play' from the beginning to the end of the Hardy novels is to detect a *volte-face* of feeling. The sympathy at the beginning is all for the white knight and heroine against the dark villain and the red-and-black villainess; but in *The Mayor* the black villain 'is already almost the hero'; in *Tess* the condemnation 'gradually shifts' from the dark villain to the blond bourgeois hero; in *Jude* the white virgin 'is the arch-sinner against life at last' (437). Thirdly, in comparing Hardy with Shakespeare again, Lawrence now puts the Shakespearian stress not on transgression against nature, but on a fatal division within the self of the hero. He still thinks Hardy's tragedies fall short of this in being caused by something outside; the aristocrats still have to die even though the direction of sympathy has been reversed. But something is stirring in the *Study*: the beginning of a new sense of duality about being and knowing, and about Hardy. The second critique is still unsatisfactory. One cannot rip characters from their context and attempt to force them into categories, and Lawrence doesn't seem to know quite what to do with his new ideas. But if there were a way to bring the 'great background' back in, and somehow to fuse *that* with the division in Hardy and a more internalised sense of character . . .?

There is a way, and Lawrence finds it by going right back to the beginning, to consider the poppy again. Only this time he opens the flower, to look inside. Chapter 6, the shortest of all, is the centre on which the whole book turns: the completion of one movement of argument; the impulsion to another. The poppy 'lives' in two ways, not one. A movement of life has sprung from seed, grown a green pillar, and then both burst into flower and held back in seed. It is both the bonfire on the edge of space, the thing at its maximum being, and (*also* in its nature) poppy-preservation, security against the future. But deeper than that, looking inside, the poppy reveals a dynamism of two 'sexual' forces in the stamens and the pistil. Both flower and seeds are the product of the clash of 'female' and 'male' – a dualism, but also a two-in-one, a creative dialectic, and this becomes a central truth for Lawrence about all life and creativity.

It is at this point in the *Study* that Lawrence's deepest concerns come together: his marriage, his struggle to write *The Wedding Ring*, his 'passionately religious' sense of the world, his thoughts about the nature of art. In Chapters 7 and 8 he tries to formulate a way of looking at all personality, relationship, religion and art as the outcome of creative conflict between two opposed forces, impersonal and universal. I shall have to summarise brutally, but some caveats may be helpful first. This burst of creative imagination is essentially *exploratory*. One must not look for the philosopher's logic or careful consistency; but one will find an extraordinary movement, and expansion, of consciousness. The thought is dialectic rather than dualistic: both forces are vital to creative growth, and the deepest concern is with the marriage and consummation, in life and art, that springs from their conflict. Though they are separable for the sake of understanding, they are ultimately one, as the movement at the rim of a wheel and the stillness at its centre are one. Lawrence is well aware that all his terminologies, female and male, the axle and the wheel, God the Father and God the Son, Law and Love, are 'arbitrary, for the purpose of thought' (448).[6] We must not translate 'male' and 'female' into 'man' and 'woman', for though the exploration begins that way, it soon becomes clear that both 'male' and 'female' forces exist and conflict within every man and woman as well as between them. 'Sex' is a fully religious mystery. On the one hand 'the sexual act . . . is for leaping off into the unknown, as from a cliff's edge' (441); on the other, sexual acts as such are not essential for laying hold of the 'beyond', and consummation may take place in the spirit as well as the body. With these cautions we may speak of the 'Female', the force of Law, of God the Father; and of the 'Male', the force of Love, of God the Son.

God the Father is immutable, stable, all-embracing, one. Life according to this Law is pure being, in complete unity with the universe of created things. Man exists in the flesh, in nature, in sensation, linked with all creation in one whole. But equally there operates throughout creation the opposite force of Love, of God the Son. This is the impulse to movement and change, from being to knowing, from undifferentiated oneness to perception of what is not-self, defining the self against the other. It is differentiation into the many, into separation, into distinct self-awareness, thought and utterance. The ideal of the Son is ever more complete individuation. The two forces are always in conflict, but the conflict is the ground of all growth. From every successive clash, in an endless process, is born a new dimension of personal life, or religion, or art. Beyond God the Father and the Son is the Holy Spirit; beyond sexual conflict is consummation, giving man and woman more completely to themselves and opening up the beyond; out of the dualism in the artist is created the work of art.

Religions express what the race or the collective consciousness aspires to, in order to complete its partiality. Men create art to utter what they know in themselves. So, both developing and testing the formulation of his dialectic, Lawrence looks at a series of particular paintings and statues. If one tries to look at them too, what may apear to be pretentious generalisations about the history of art or the psychic states of artists turn out to be remarkably precise and illuminating perceptions. The central quality of the 'Madonna with the Iris',[7] 'in the style of' Dürer, is how completely she occupies the picture in 'stable, incontrovertible being' (456). Plants and butterflies in her rustic bower (hardly distinguished from nature), and the suckling child which is an extension of her, all unite in togetherness with her tranquil centrality. But Botticelli's 'Mystic Nativity'[8] is a marvellous fusion of stability with ecstatic movement, centrifugal with centripetal force. At the still centre is the child. But, as one looks again, the child is in motion. The curious pose of the father, 'folded up' like a boulder (455), pulls the eye round to the right; the statuesque mother pushes it round to the left, suggesting a circular movement around Him. The angels clasping humans at the foot of the picture are both frozen in a moment of communion, and seem about to turn in dance. The four planes of the picture from bottom to top initiate movement, spiring and counterspiring, which culminates in the joyous whirl of angels at the top, but the painting is *composed* about a still centre, tranquil. In 'Dürer's' picture God the Father predominates; in Botticelli's the Father is 'married' to the Son. Raphael and Michelangelo intensify in opposite directions. In Raphael's 'Ansidei Madonna'[9] the Virgin and Child are oddly abstracted-looking; but he 'rings her round with pure geometry, till she becomes herself almost of the geometric figure, an abstraction. The picture becomes a great ellipse crossed by a dark column' (460). It is still a marriage of 'male' and 'female', the column and the ellipse, but though there is unity and stability, almost static, it is produced by an act of abstract mind. But if Raphael is 'the male reacting upon itself' (458) creating abstraction, Michelangelo 'sought the female in himself, aggrandized it, and so reached a wonderful momentary stability of flesh exaggerated till it became tenuous, but filled and balanced by the outward-pressing force'. So, the Moses looms 'announcing, like the Jewish God, the magnificence and eternality of the physical law'; the David is 'young, but with too much body for a young figure, the physique exaggerated, the clear, outward-leaping, essential spirit of the young man smothered over'; the slaves heave in body 'fastened in bondage that refuses them movement', the Adam on the Sistine ceiling 'can scarcely stir into life. That large body of almost transparent, tenuous texture is not established enough for motion', yet it is not motion he requires, but body. 'Give him but a firm, concentrated physique. That is the cry of all Michelangelo's pictures' (462). Yet other constations of the forces are to be found in

Correggio, Rembrandt, and Turner. In the 'Madonna of the Basket'[10] the Virgin has become secular, a natural young girl with her baby and her workbasket, while her husband carpenters in the background. Correggio is concerned not with 'her great female mystery, but her individual character' (456). She is almost a woman he knows, though there is still a hint of mystery, a strange light and expressiveness in her face and in the stretch of the child to something beyond. In Rembrandt the light of knowledge is turned on to the flesh in increasing individuality. The human being is a separate self, distinct, 'and he must study himself . . . So Rembrandt paints his own portrait again and again, sees it again and again within the light.' But though this is a great act of progressive individuation it is also more. 'It is the declaration that light is our medium of existence, that where the light falls upon our darkness there we *are* : that I am but the point where light and darkness meet and break upon one another' (471). So the light is also the light of the spirit which in 'The Jewish Bride'[11] or even in the 'Portrait of Himself and Saskia',[12] the man looks towards, past the embrace with the woman. And in the late portraits the light both enables individuality to materialise in every wrinkle, and is itself made manifest. But Turner 'did not seek to mate body with spirit . . . what he sought was the mating of the Spirit . . . Ever, he sought the Light, to make the light transfuse the body, till the body was carried away.' Turner's final picture might have been a pure white incandescent surface, but 'such a picture as his *Norham Castle, Sunrise,*[13] where only the faintest shadow of life stains the light, is the last word that can be uttered, before the blazing and timeless silence' (474). But, Lawrence adds, 'I cannot look at a later Turner picture without abstracting myself, without denying that I have limbs . . . If I look at the Norham Castle and remember my own knees and my own breast, then the picture is a nothing to me' (475). What he looks for is an art in which all the contraries are married, not affirmed at one another's expense.

Critics of both Lawrence and Hardy have tended to shy away from the art-criticism in the *Study*, yet it is crucially important in enabling Lawrence to return to Hardy in an altogether deeper dimension, and to judge by the highest standards. In the art-criticism the 'ideas' have been authenticated, the contraries shown to be actually there in works of art. But in the process the multiplicities of creative tension have been revealed as far more complex than the dialectic theory itself could have suggested. So, in getting down to Hardy for the third time, the earlier positions have to be subsumed, complicated, deepened. The 'great background' can no longer be merely a background or a single life-force, for it has been *internalised* in the conflict of opposed forces of nature *within the self* and in *relationship*. It cannot be 'more important' (or less) than the people who move 'upon it', for universal forces have been so fused with character and into relationship that the classifications of the 'aristocrats' and the dichotomy of individual and community have become far too simple. The author's division is the ground of creativity; and it is the tension of opposed forces within characters – the Shakespearian mode from which Hardy had previously been excluded – and between them, that now holds all the attention. The stress must fall on *Tess* and *Jude*.

But what kind of criticism emerges? Lawrence formulates expectations for Tess that Hardy doesn't voice; and the way she is seen as destroyed by the opposite imbalances of Alec and Angel leaves aside the contingencies of the narrative. Yet the X-ray diagnosis is essentially true, both to one's sense of the stature of Tess, and to the basic impression the novel leaves on the memory long after the details have gone. This is because of the new sureness with which Lawrence cuts right through the dimensions of behaviour, and even feeling and self-consciousness – both the older morality of conduct and the newer morality of sensibility – to the fundamental nature of Hardy's people; and because Hardy's art was moving in the same direction. So the characteristics and the actions of Alec and Angel become symptoms of intrinsic imbalance in their natures, indeed of radical insufficiency of self through the atrophy of one or other of the essential natural drives. Alec will inevitably seek Tess for self-gratification, since (though masculine enough) he lacks the 'male' drive to discover a further dimension of selfhood through what is beyond himself. He is bound to see Tess 'as the embodied fulfilment of his own desire: something, that is, belonging to him. She cannot, in his conception, exist apart from him nor have any being apart from his being' (483). It is inevitable that Angel will deeply despise the woman in her, substitute ideas for her, desert her to go wandering, because of the atrophy in himself of all that Law, the 'female', has come to mean. Whereas Tess, intrinsic 'female', also has the 'male' respect for the Other, never seeing others as extensions of herself or herself as the centre of the universe, but accepting herself, and others, as they are. This is a big quality, more than passivity or fatalism. It helps to explain a reader's respect for Tess, and his feeling that she deserves a full 'consummation' of her complex human potentialities. To appreciate the depth of Alec's betrayal of her *being* is to see the murder as deeply credible, however clumsily managed; but also to see why no full life is possible with Angel, even apart from policemen and the law. As Lawrence moves from *Tess* to *Jude*, however, he does more than extend his previous analysis. He begins by noting the parallel between Alec and Arabella; though he also argues very acutely that they are intrinsically bigger than the materialisation Hardy allows in the *nouveau-riche* cad, or in the false hair and the practised dimple. (This is clear from the great scenes, on the harvester, or the pig-killing, where they demonstrably have a stature and a pressure they are often denied elsewhere.) He goes on to show Jude, both 'male' and 'female', pulled apart between Arabella and Sue as Tess had been between Alec and Angel. What is new, however, is the way Lawrence grows to see Jude as contributing to his own tragedy. Having realised half of himself through Arabella he is only too willing to deny it, wanting 'to arrest all his activity in his mind' (495) and being drawn inevitably to Sue. Yet the tragedy with Sue is very different. The previous logic suggests that, having 'produced an individual flower of his own' (499) through his 'male' relationship with Sue, it was natural that he should also want to sleep with, and have children by her. Yet Lawrence's critical imagination, responding with increasing compassion and understanding, sees more deeply into the radical incapacity in Hardy's Sue which rendered the sexual relationship fatal, and the death of the children artistically inevitable. He cuts through the 'bisexuality' of Sue (in ordinary terms) to a deeper and more accurate perception of a highly specialised being-in-one-kind, who is as surely destroyed by Jude's blind dragging 'his body after his consciousness' as he is by her. Jude and Sue 'are damned, partly by their very being, but chiefly by their incapacity to accept the conditions of their own and each other's being' (505). The change from the 'aristocrat' section, where she is the arch-sinner against life, is very marked. 'Sue had a being, special and beautiful. Why must not Jude recognize it in all its speciality? . . . She was not "a woman". She was Sue Bridehead, something very particular. Why was there no place for her?' (510).

It is because, Lawrence concludes, Hardy came at the end of an epoch of the supremacy of God the Son. Deeply drawn to the opposite world of the older Law, Hardy feared it and tended always to write it down – hence Alec, Arabella and their predecessors. His art had moved, ever more surely, to assert the impulse to individuation in mind and spirit, denying the body which unites man with the natural universe. But Hardy could only pit one force *against* the other, tragically; he could see no possible reconciliation. What remained to strive for was a 'supreme fiction' in which both sides of the dialectic would have full expression, neither overbalancing the other; but in which there would also be 'the final reconciliation, where both are equal, two in one, complete' (516). As Lawrence began, at once, to rewrite *The Wedding Ring* into *The Rainbow*, that was his aim.

His dialogue with Hardy finally brought about the revolutionary change in his own fiction he had struggled so hard to achieve. By exploring Hardy's people he had found a language in which to articulate his vision; and also, as I have argued elsewhere,[14] the outlines of a new structure for the first of the two novels (not one) that would be needed. The *Study* showed him how to begin, how to divide *The Rainbow* into its three 'testaments', and where to end in near-tragedy, but with a vision of reconciliation to be achieved in the second novel. It also awakened images which his novelist's imagination could explore in terms of human relationship, with marvellous sensitivity and insight.[15] But above all, his experience of Hardy must have been the greatest possible authentication and encouragement of his own vision. Here, of all English novelists, was one who saw human life against a vast impersonal landscape, and whose characters already existed in terms of being and consciousness rather than the conduct and sensibility of 'the old stable ego'.[16] As he pondered more deeply he had come to see how, as Hardy's fiction developed, the great background had become internalised in the conflict of universal forces within the characters themselves, at such a depth that they already clarified, in credibly human complexity, the interplay of contraries which he had been trying to understand in his own life and art. Yet he must have felt – the most liberating perception of affinity – that Hardy had neither seen clearly where he was going nor gone far enough, that there was room to move beyond him and, above all, to move beyond his pessimism. What *Tess* and *Jude* began, *The Rainbow* could complete.

Yet the very depth and clarity of his insight shows up the limitations of its focus. He took one dimension of Hardy criticism as far as it would go; but in so doing he poses, all the more sharply because of his affinity with the most 'Lawrentian' of the Wessex novels, the challenge to pin down the other dimensions he seems blind to, but which make Hardy himself, and not an incomplete D. H. Lawrence. Significantly, *The Mayor of Casterbridge* is hardly there in the *Study* and everything implied by 'of Casterbridge' is underplayed: Hardy's stubborn sense of how unavoidably 'character' is conditioned and action limited by place and time, by being-in-society and being-in-history. The way a Hardy character is himself must also be the way in which he locates an interplay of economic conditions, social mores, a past which is a living presence, and the history-within-the-blood. Lawrence can show the inevitability of the death of Sue's children in one sense, because of what their parents are in themselves; but he largely ignores the multiple pressures of place and history which brought them where they are, and the tragically foreshortened sense of Time that names the executioner. One must be careful here: the complex ways in which *The Rainbow* is a social history will show that Lawrence was not as single-minded as he seems in the *Study*.

Yet always his drive is to free his characters from society and history, determining themselves. For Lawrence, Hardy's sense of limitation is an imaginative failure; for Hardy, Lawrence's sense of freedom would be delusion. This is an opposition so radical that it must give rise to fundamentally different kinds of art. If I have used the X-ray metaphor for Lawrence's criticism, it was to suggest his search 'beneath the surface' for some basic structure in art and life. But Hardy's whole way of seeing is different: if a Hardy novel is a 'series of seemings' or a 'great web', it is because no single way of seeing will do. Vision, to be inclusive enough, must be from this angle, *and* that, *and* this; and the multiple perspectives do not fuse so much as sustain one another by a sense of interweaving. Hardy is more tentative, more aware of how one way of looking is different from as well as linked to another, more sceptical. He is also more aware of multiplicity, and of the sheer difficulty of seeing enough and of holding what one sees together. (It was probably the erosion by the late 1890s of the possibility of using 'Wessex' as an *externally* coherent world any longer that made Hardy abandon fiction.) The 'series of seemings' has to be articulated by a Narrative which both allows for accident and holds design; and which, in moving narrator and reader from one location and mode of observation to another, never allows point-of-view to settle. Where Lawrence tends to be immersed in and committed to everything he writes, Hardy moves in and out of his fiction, now sympathetically involved, now wryly distanced, shifting stance from sentence to sentence or even within a sentence. No two novelists, in being so like each other, are in fact so different.

'Where *Jude* ends, *The Rainbow* begins.'[17] This is true both in the sense in which, together, they mark the change from nineteenth-century to modern, from the novel of behaviour to the novel of being, from character to consciousness; and also in the sense in which Hardy helped Lawrence to find himself, and carry to completion what he saw in the Wessex novels. Yet it is no less important to see how, and why, Hardy 'ends' with *Jude*. Indeed Lawrence's own dialectic gives one the final clue to the significance of his study of Hardy, in emphasising how both the 'self' and the 'other' are 'singled out' in themselves, through the discovery of true relationship.

NOTES

1   *Phoenix – The Posthumous Papers of D. H. Lawrence*, ed. E. D. McDonald (London, 1936) pp. 398–516. Page references in the text are to this edition. The *Study* is now also available in *Lawrence on Hardy and Painting*, ed. J. V. Davies (London, 1973).

2   To Pinker, 5 September 1914: 'What a miserable world. What colossal idiocy, this war. Out of sheer rage I've begun my book about Thomas

Hardy.' *The Collected Letters of D. H. Lawrence*, ed. Harry T. Moore (London, 1962) I, p. 290; hereafter referred to as 'C.L.'. Lawrence told Amy Lowell on 18 November that he was almost finished – S. Foster Damon, *Amy Lowell. A Chronicle* (Boston, 1935) p. 279 – and, later, that it had 'turned out as a sort of Story of My Heart, or a *Confessio Fidei*' – C.L. 298. For a fuller account of the circumstances of composition of the *Study* and its relation to the making of *The Rainbow* and *Women in Love*, see Mark Kinkead-Weekes, 'The Marble and the Statue' in *Imagined Worlds*, ed. Maynard Mack and Ian Gregor (London, 1968) pp. 371–418.

3 C.L. 273. In a 'Foreword to Sons and Lovers', written in January 1913 and never meant for publication, he had first attempted to rewrite Christian theology in terms of the relation of man and woman. See *The Letters of D. H. Lawrence*, ed. Aldous Huxley (London, 1932) pp. 95–102.

4 T. S. Eliot, *Notes towards the Definition of Culture* (London, 1948) p. 21.

5 C.L. 289. Methuen claimed later to have returned the manuscript because 'it could not be published in its then condition' – see the report of proceedings at the trial of *The Rainbow*, *Sunday Times*, 14 November 1915, p. 13. There is evidence however that many publishing ventures were being retrenched because of the war. In a moment, the financial security of Methuen's lucrative offer had turned into serious embarrassment for the Lawrences.

6 As if to mark the point, Lawrence reversed 'male' and 'female' in the opening pages of *The Rainbow*. I prefer the terminology of God the Father and the Son as less liable to misunderstanding.

7 In the National Gallery, London (the lower gallery).

8 In the National Gallery, London.

9 In the National Gallery, London.

10 In the National Gallery, London.

11 In the Rijksmuseum, Amsterdam.

12 In the Pinakotek, Dresden.

13 In the Tate Gallery, London.

14 'The Marble and the Statue', op. cit., pp. 380–6.

15 For example, the use of the axle and the wheel in the chapter on the honeymoon of Anna and Will; the expansion of the *Study*'s remarks on medieval cathedrals and on the column and ellipse in the Cathedral chapter; the pervasive exploration of Rembrandtesque light and dark; the Turneresque incandescence in the scene with Skrebensky on the beach.

16 C.L. 282. The *Study* helps us, as it helped Lawrence, to grasp what he had been struggling to say in this letter. In *The Rainbow*, Ursula does pass through 'allotropic states' in which, while still recognisably Ursula, she seems radically different; as she is patterned in different ways by differing interactions of the 'male' and 'female' forces within and upon her, in the successive phases of her story.

17 The final sentence in Ian Gregor, *The Great Web* (London, 1974).

9 Either Side of Wessex

Michael Irwin and Ian Gregor

I

'The following novel, the first published by the author, was written nineteen years ago, at a time when he was feeling his way to a method.'

Hardy is writing a preface for *Desperate Remedies*, and looking back, in the manner of an author secure in his achievement, at problems now happily resolved. For Hardy, writing in 1889, such an attitude was appropriate and understandable. For us, the longer perspective makes the position appear differently.

This is particularly true now that the New Wessex Edition has restored the 'minor' novels to general currency. Looking at the line of fiction that extends a quarter of a century from *Desperate Remedies* (1871) to *The Well-Beloved* (1897) we can see that there never was a time when Hardy ceased 'feeling his way to a method'. Critical concentration on the six famous 'Wessex' novels has made his art appear simpler and more homogeneous than it was. To study the minor works is to be reminded that Hardy's creative talents involved tensions and contrarieties not easily or always reconciled in fictional terms.

By examining the beginning and the end of Hardy's career as a novelist we hope to show why he might have found it peculiarly difficult to evolve a 'method', why his method should have led him to the idea of Wessex, and why that idea should finally have been abandoned in the interests of an apparently new development. It is not our present purpose to attempt a revaluation of the minor novels, but at least, and unquestionably, *Desperate Remedies* can tell us a great deal about Hardy's early aims and problems, and *The Well-Beloved* can enlarge our understanding of *Jude*. Our central concern, however, is not with this or that particular novel, but with Hardy's own imaginative journey – a voyage of exploration that neither began nor ended in Wessex.

II

Hardy himself was to say of *Desperate Remedies* that 'the powerfully, not to say wildly, melodramatic situations had been concocted in a style which was quite against his natural grain . . .' But the modern reader who comes to this first novel from the later ones finds not merely an excellent tale of mystery and suspense but a work which is in its very texture Hardyesque. There is a singularity in the descriptive writing that reveals a distinctive imagination, a distinctive vision. The author is already following his own later prescript: '. . . the seer should watch that pattern among general things which his idiosyncrasy moves him to observe, and describe that alone.'

His own 'idiosyncrasy' is perhaps best illustrated from the *Life*, where he is free to write for himself. In the course of a long illness he makes this note:

January 13. Incidents of lying in bed for months. Skin gets fair: corns take their leave: feet and toes grow shapely as those of a Greek statue. Keys get rusty; watch dim, boots mildewed; hat and clothes old-fashioned; umbrella eaten out with rust; children seen through the window are grown taller.

The entry is striking in several ways. Hardy has found in particularities a very effective notation for an abstract experience. The sights he records are individually pleasing in their unexpectedness, but gain force from juxtaposition. A variety of aspects of living are brought into implied connection; decay and regeneration are curiously linked. Somehow the bare factual memorandum comes to suggest a view of life. As an account of a serious illness the passage is at the same time intensely personal and intensely impersonal.

In *Desperate Remedies*, too, Hardy frequently chooses to isolate – to focus attention on, say, a single hair from Mrs Manston's head, or a single raindrop, or 'a warm foot in a polished boot'. The same habit leads him to define scenes by means of salient detail: '. . . their clothing touched, and remained in contact'; 'The shovel shone like silver from the action of the juice . . .' At a further stage of reduction many an incident is sketched solely in sounds: '. . . the click of the smoke-jack, the flap of the flames, and the light touches of the women's slippers upon the stone floor.' Repeatedly Hardy looks at an ordinary place or landscape from an unusual angle, or sees it under an unusual aspect. The palings in Lincoln's Inn Fields are 'rusted away at their base to the thinness of wires'. Conversely, in a dramatic frost Cytherea sees that 'A shoot of the diameter of a pin's head was iced as thick as her finger . . .' Scene after scene is brilliantly coloured, or is distinctively lit by sun, moon, candle, lantern, firelight or match.

As in the extract quoted from the *Life* the descriptive habit implies a habit of thought, a stance towards experience. There is a constant attempt to present the familiar in a new guise – to make the reader look with fresh eyes and see unsuspected relationships. On the merely stylistic level the same instinct is seen in the surprising similes: 'countless stars fluttering like bright birds'; 'high-hipped, rich-coloured cows with backs horizontal and straight as the ridge of a house'; 'her small taper fingers extended like the leaves of a lupine.' At the narrative level the oddity of vision can be dramatised within the episode. For conveniently hyperbolic examples we must look beyond *Desperate Remedies*. In *A Pair of Blue Eyes* Elfride undressing on the cliff-top, Knight hanging from the cliff-face, Smith sailing home from Egypt and a fossil some millions of years old are brought into a pattern of mutual regard. In *The Well-Beloved* Pierston takes in at one view Avice's moving coffin 'with its twelve legs', a church, a lighthouse, the sea and even the twinkle of a school of mackerel.

It is not, perhaps, immediately apparent that these various practices involve a tension, or even a contradiction. They express not a single tendency but two opposed tendencies. One is towards vividness, immediacy. There is a sense of being brought into direct contact with a certain sight or sound. Yet at the same time the peculiarity of the perspective, or the almost 'metaphysical' quality of the simile, can seem deliberately obtrusive – designed, not to present the thing itself, but an attitude to, or an idea about, that thing. Again, the extravagance of Hardy's visual effects is no more characteristic than a countervailing precision: 'she acquired perceptions of the newcomer in the following order: unknown trousers; unknown waistcoat; unknown face.' Altogether Hardy's 'idiosyncrasy of regard' involves a series of opposites: immediacy against detachment, spontaneity against reflection, flamboyance against formality. Such antinomies are ingeniously reconciled in Hardy's incidental perceptions – are indeed the very thing that makes them intriguing; but it might be suspected that in a developed story antagonistic intentions might lead the author into difficulty.

That is a question to which we will return. When he was writing *Desperate Remedies* Hardy was necessarily concerned with the more basic problem of whether his descriptive skills were appropriate to fiction at all. Would he be able to do more than work into his narrative arresting visual material taken, as it might be, from a commonplace book? From our vantage-point we might pose the

question differently: Hardy's art is often called cinematographic –
might not *Desperate Remedies* be compared to the work of a director
prolix in stark images and novel camera-angles, but with nothing
much to say? Are style and subject-matter brought into relationship?
Is the novel more than a mystery-story with descriptive decorations?

A defence of its unity of purpose might begin from the fact that
the scenes Hardy describes often alter the mood or motive of those
who witness them. After Cytherea has rejected Manston's advances
he is walking in his back-yard and turns to look into a water-
butt:

> Hundreds of thousands of minute living creatures sported and
> tumbled in its depths with every contortion that gaiety could
> suggest; perfectly happy, though consisting only of a head, or a
> tail, or at most a head and a tail, and all doomed to die within
> the twenty-four hours.

This is pure Hardy: it isn't easy to think of another novelist who
would describe the contents of a water-butt. But the passage is no
mere interlude. Manston is affected by what he sees: 'Damn my
position! Why shouldn't I be happy through my little day too? Let
the parish sneer at my repulses, let it. I'll get her, If I move heaven
and earth to do it!'

Shortly afterwards, when he is renewing his advances to Cytherea,
her tendency to submit to them is partly traceable to the effects of
her surroundings, a meadow at sunset:

> The stillness oppressed and reduced her to mere passivity. The
> only wish the humidity of the place left in her was to stand
> motionless. The helpless flatness of the landscape gave her, as it
> gives all such temperaments, a sense of bare equality with, and
> no superiority to, a single entity under the sun.

It must be admitted that these effects are local ones. The characters
of Manston and Cytherea are insufficiently developed to permit any
real latitude of motive. In any case the plot requires that they must
behave as they do were the landscape hilly and Manston's water-butt
empty. But Hardy is surely not just demonstrating his 'idiosyncrasy
of regard' but already 'feeling his way' towards the creation of a
context that will give it narrative relevance. When he uses again,
in *The Return of the Native*, the passage about the effect of a flat
landscape it takes on far greater significance, but significance of a
similar kind.

There is an interesting congruity between the unlikely relation of character and background suggested by such episodes and the unlikely relationships implied by Hardy's strange images and tricks of perspective. Both story and description deal in curious links, resemblances, affinities, influences. The freaks of nature – sudden storms or frosts, for instance – parallel the freakishness of human conduct. The fire which destroys the Three Tranters is necessary to Hardy's plot; but as he describes it, circumstantially, from its minutest beginnings it could be a metaphor for the accidentally initiated destructiveness of Manston. Both in substructure and in superstructure *Desperate Remedies* demonstrates the strangeness and the interconnectedness of the world.

Such a summary might suggest that Hardy the novelist would find matter and manner in easy harmony. But in fact it embodies the very contradiction mentioned earlier. 'Strangeness' pulls one way, 'interconnectedness' the other. Again extravagance and pattern are in conflict. The problem becomes clearer if one goes beyond detail and incident to look at a complete episode. A useful example to analyse might be that of Mr Graye's death; partly because it is the first directly-narrated episode in the novel, partly because it is gratuitous. Mr Graye could be disposed of as summarily as his unfortunate wife: a heart-attack would seem the obvious and humane way of eliminating him. Instead Hardy has him fall off a church-tower in full view of his daughter. The manner of his death has no consequences in the story: it seems solely designed to provide a lurid start.

Yet in the telling the episode is *not* lurid. Neither Cytherea nor the reader sees Mr Graye hit the ground: he merely disappears downwards. His death, like the others in *Desperate Remedies* – like the great majority of deaths in Hardy – takes place *just* off-stage. But a more important factor is stylisation. Hardy is at pains to formalise the picture Cytherea see from the Town Hall:

> It was an illuminated miniature, framed in by the dark margin of the window, the keen-edged shadiness of which emphasised by contrast the softness of the objects enclosed.

Naturally the men on top of the steeple are physically diminished. They 'appeared little larger than pigeons, and made their tiny movements with a soft, spirit-like stillness.' Another kind of distancing effect is achieved by Hardy's comment on Cytherea, who is idly looking on: 'as listless and careless as one of the ancient Tarentines, who, on such an afternoon as this, watched from the Theatre the entry into their Harbour of a power that overturned the State'.

Having devised a needlessly sensational episode, then, Hardy makes it carefully, almost pedantically, unsensational. The 'framing' device he uses here he later, of course, resorts to again and again. It neatly figures the author's instinctive subjection of narrative or descriptive extravagance to control.

Already in *Desperate Remedies* there are signs of a spasmodic attempt by Hardy to discipline his plot, too, by patterning. Miss Aldclyffe is made to see herself and Cytherea as counterparts: each of them falling in love with a man who is already engaged. But she herself is a counterpart to Edward Springrove, in that for each the course of true love is obstructed by premature entanglement with a cousin. From this point of view Cytherea's plight corresponds to her father's and is only a mirror-image of Miss Aldclyffe's. There is further parallelism between Cytherea and Edward, as they are simultaneously drawn towards undesired marriages through unselfish willingness to help a relative.

If Hardy had gone further in this direction he might have groped his way towards a very modern kind of novel: the kind in which structural symmetries signal to the reader that extravagances of plot are meant to have a figurative, not a literal force. The kind of novel, in fact, that Iris Murdoch writes. Already in *A Pair of Blue Eyes* Hardy produces at least a near-success in just such a mode. Yet this is not the line that he chooses to follow; and it is intriguing to speculate why.

One obvious reason is that over a large area of his interests Hardy was predominantly a realist. Authenticity is natural to his descriptive mode. He does not lightly invoke fire or storm: he knows how a blaze starts and what noises wind and rain make. He knows about landscape, local history, geology, dialect, work. The *Life* shows that the kind of anecdote he liked to record combined the unusual or even the melodramatic with just such authenticity. The characteristic narrative impulse is not: 'There was once a man who sold his wife – ', but rather: 'There was once a hay-trusser named Henchard who sold his wife in a drunken fit at Weydon Fair.' Such a story is, of course, highly recalcitrant to patterning. The unusualness might be retained, but the authenticity will be lost.

But, as often in discussion of Hardy's art, the general statement needs immediate qualification. This authenticity is itself limited. Hardy sees vividly, but sees as a detached observer – through a window, through a keyhole, from the summit of a hill. The vision tends to be static – less a film than a sequence of slides. Some things he fails to see at all. The on-stage doings of Hardy's major characters may be sharply specific; by contrast their off-stage and antecedent lives can be so shadowy as to be almost unimaginable. Almost every novel has some markedly theoretical aspect. Manston is the first of a long line of characters who try to regulate their conduct in terms of a private system of belief or disbelief. In a substantial, working, rural world these theoreticians are alien figures in more senses than Hardy intended. Throughout his career he was to hesitate between the predominant realism and a formalism that might accommodate such visitors. There is often a sense, even in his greatest novels, of ideas extrinsic to the story that is being told, or of vivid episodes that have yet drifted away from significance or control.

III

The context that brought 'the ideas' and 'the story' into a relationship to be sustained through most of Hardy's career as a novelist came into being with *Far from the Madding Crowd*. It was, of course, Wessex. In a preface written twenty years after the novel Hardy says that he envisaged 'a series of novels . . . requiring a territorial definition of some sort to lend unity to the scene.' The kind of unity involved however, is not so simply described. 'Wessex' enabled Hardy to shift his narrative stance slightly, but crucially, so that he was freed from a manner of narration which suggested the inventor of tales, to a manner which suggested he was their chronicler. He was able to convey a sense of time which was suggestive both of the historian and 'The Shepheardes Calendar'. Fact and fiction could be brought into a new relationship. If there was melodrama in Wessex it was because there was a melodrama in nature, in the sudden violence of storm and fire, or because it invaded our workaday lives when a prosperous shepherd could be rendered destitute by the sudden self-destruction of his sheep, or our emotional lives because the gargoyles of some churches in Wessex are sadly in need of repair. This glaze of circumstantiality laid upon a fiction is present in the first thing we encounter in every Wessex novel – the map. We see a region immediately recognisable in outline and contour, but wholly fictive in name; a region with a history but peopled by romance. Hardy had created an imagined world in which contraries could coexist. If 'detail' could be endlessly accommodated in the texture of that world, in woods and heath and trackways, in methods of work, in the business of the market-place, in the pleasures of the ale house, 'pattern' could find expression in its structure, in the rhythm of the seasons, in simple plots about three men and a girl, about fickle soldiery and abandoned serving girls. It allows, too, a place for the ubiquitous observer, labelled variously 'a wayfarer' or 'a bystander', to overhear voices in the dark or behind a wall, to glimpse people moving in the shadows or framed suddenly in a window or a doorway, and by an accumulation of such impressions to be able to convey a sense of a whole community being looked at and appraised by a vigilant eye.

As originally conceived, however, this 'world' had a crucial limitation which Hardy soon recognised: it could make his work narrow and stereotyped. 'He was aware of the pecuniary value of a reputation for a speciality . . . yet he had not the slightest intention of writing for ever about sheepfarming, as the reading public was apparently expecting him to do, and as, in fact, they presently resented his not doing.'[1] It was in the process of writing *The Return of the Native*, with the introduction of Clym, that Hardy realised that Wessex need no longer be thought of as 'writing about sheepfarming', but, in Matthew Arnold's phrase, could be made to include 'the dialogue of the mind with itself'. Into Wessex Hardy was able to introduce not simply the structure provided by indigenous customs and plots, but more inclusively, the structure of a contemporary consciousness, ambivalent in its sympathies and sceptical in outlook. The development of Wessex could, in other words, be made commensurate with the development of the author.

As Hardy's novels developed in the 1880s we see him continuing 'to extend his method', but comfortably within the frontiers set by Wessex. Emphases change, but the basic pattern remains. In form, a contemplative narrator broods over a community evoked in loving detail; in substance, the narrative is structured in major conflicts, Henchard against Farfrae, Grace against Melbury and Giles, Angel against Tess. But that very sequence of names indicates the change overcoming Wessex, which was to be more than a change of emphasis. The region is becoming as much an interior landscape as an external one. If we compare the presentation of Weatherbury Farm with Talbothays we see the nature of the shift. Perhaps no landscape in Hardy is presented with more scrupulous care and loving attention to detail than the farm which Tess enjoys as a milkmaid, but if we compare it with Weatherbury, we recognise that the feeling it evokes is inseparable from the love of Angel and Tess; and behind that lie the feelings of an author who knows that his idyll is really an elegy. Wessex, as it goes through successive presentations, becomes gradually more and more stylised, the region shaped increasingly by the feelings of the author and by the invading of a world elsewhere. When Tess dies – the last and richest embodiment of the region – Wessex dies too.

But Hardy, like Angel Clare, has to 'go on', to write a fiction that will express those feelings about isolation, about love, about the modern world, which were released by Wessex and came finally to overwhelm it. The challenge was to find a method to express the contraries which had haunted his imagination but without the support which the rural background had given him for so long.

IV

Fitzpiers and Angel Clare are obliged to adjust their different brands of romantic idealism to the demands of the real world. In *The Well-Beloved* modern, self-conscious man, the theoretician, is examined on his own terms. The result is by definition a formal, patterned novel. Hardy stylises into new significance what seems at first to be a familiar situation. The concentration is on Jocelyn Pierston and on 'the lonely rock of his birthplace' where he seeks his beloved. It is the return of the native again – with a difference. Clym comes 'home' to find 'some rational occupation among the people I know best'; Jocelyn's only 'home' is in peace of mind, his occupation, so far from being 'among people', is the product of his own imagination, carved out of the rock of his birthplace and shaped into art by the frustrations of his solitary life. The novel is the tale of a self-enclosure which lasts a lifetime; this native is not estranged from his birthplace, but from himself.

To convey the intensity and the duration of this self-dislocation, Hardy puts into practice a prescription he wrote in his notebook at the begining of 1893. 'The whole secret of fiction and the drama – in the constructional part – lies in the adjustment of things unusual to things eternal and universal.' In *The Well-Beloved* 'things unusual' are juxtaposed to 'things eternal' with stark severity. The story of the Sculptor, with a metropolitan reputation, in love with three generations of girls from the same family is seen against a background of Hardy's profoundly held beliefs about the nature of love and the inexorable passing of time. To facilitate 'the constructional part' Hardy availed himself of the Platonic belief in the transmigration of the beloved. This was the machinery which enabled him, as he puts it, 'to introduce the subjective theory of love into modern fiction'. Without interrogating that phrase too closely, its direction can be felt if we compare the difference in emphasis of Arnold's phrase 'the dialogue of the mind with itself' when applied to *The Return of the Native* and then to *The Well-Beloved*.

By laying the emphasis so firmly on the interiorisation of *The Well-Beloved*, it might seem that we are overlooking 'the island' as presenting a substantial reality which is indifferent to Jocelyn's dilemma. In a sense, the 'treeless rock' does have a function similar to Egdon, it too is 'a face upon which time makes little impression' and provides therefore an ironic counterpoint to the characters. But where 'the vast tract of unenclosed land' has a reality quite independent of the drama acted out upon it, the Isle of Slingers, vivid and detailed as it is, has about it a hallucinatory clarity reminiscent of expressionist films:

The towering rock, the houses above houses, one man's doorstep rising behind his neighbour's chimney, the gardens hung up by one edge to the sky, the vegetables growing on apparently almost vertical planes, the unity of the whole island as a solid and single block of limestone four miles long, were no longer familiar and commonplace ideas. All now stood dazzlingly unique and white against the tinted sea, and the sun flashed on infinitely stratified walls of oolite . . . with a distinctiveness that called the eyes to it as strongly as any spectacle he had beheld afar.

For all the visual sharpness of that scene, it is the observer we are finally reminded of, and when later, Jocelyn sees the huge cubes of white oolite on the wharves of the Thames, we feel the landscape has moved and begun to acquire the 'insubstantiality of the well-beloved'.

If the construction of *The Well-Beloved* enables Hardy to present in fiction the idea of love with the directness we associate with his poetry and to dramatise in the character of Jocelyn, a subjective awareness of that idea, it also allows him to convey something further: the sense of the passage of time.

The fantasy of the plot allows the lapse of time to operate in two ways which seem at first almost antithetical. The repetition of the drama over three generations with Jocelyn and Avice Caro gives the sense of a universal predicament, a dilemma intrinsic in man's emotional aspirations, where the reach and the grasp are always at odds. In that perspective the successive generations give the sense of duration, of endless sequence; in another perspective the very similarity of the drama within each generation telescopes them, so that they become aspects of a single conflict. But whichever way we look, these two perspectives are united in a third which sees the process of time as endlessly destructive. We have the tension and pathos expressed in the titles of each part of the novel, 'A Young Man of Twenty', 'A Young Man of Forty', 'A Young Man of Sixty', and succinctly, in a poem of the same period.

> But Time, to make me grieve,
> Part steals, lets part abide;
> And shakes this fragile frame at eve
> With throbbings of noontide.

Time is destructive but it is sadly teasing too; it is only when Jocelyn looks at himself in the mirror or looks at Marcia that the full force of Time's passage is seen:

She stood the image and superscription of Age – an old woman, pale and shrivelled, her forehead ploughed, her cheek hollow, her hair white as snow. To this the face he once kissed had been brought by the raspings, chisellings, scourgings, bakings, freezings of forty invidious years – by the thinkings of more than half a life-time.

It would be false to the spirit of *The Well-Beloved* to leave an account of it, however brief, on that bleak and uncompromising note. It would be false because when Hardy was 'feeling for a method' he needed the distance which fantasy would bring not only to reveal the tragedy in Jocelyn's situation, but also to release the comic spirit which, for Hardy, kept it close company. It is a spirit which 'surprises Jocelyn into stillness', when Avice the second, the least attractive and intelligent of the girls, says by way of explaining her resistance to his advances, 'I have loved *fifteen* a'ready! Yes, fifteen I am almost ashamed to say', she repeated laughing. 'I can't help it, sir, I assure you. Of course, it is really to *me*, the same one all through, only I can't catch him . . .' That Avice should be allowed to state the theme so bluntly suggests that Hardy was nicely aware that *The Well-Beloved*, for all its seriousness, should keep a modest sense of its scope.

The modesty consists, in its abstract construction, in the sense that this is *merely* a novel of pattern, that Love, Art and Time seek to be spelt with capital letters and exist virtually outside a context of historical circumstance. To restore that context became Hardy's aim as he turned Jocelyn into Jude, the well-beloved into Sue, and 'the lonely island' into Christminster and elsewhere. Through the obliquities of *The Well-Beloved* Hardy had prepared himself for a more direct treatment of the idea of love, so that he now felt ready to write, as he says in his preface, 'a novel addressed by a man to men and women of full age; which attempts to deal unaffectedly with the fret and fear, derision and disaster, that may press in the wake of the strongest passion known to humanity; to tell, without a mincing of words, of a deadly war waged between flesh and spirit . . .' Hardy had never been more passionate, more direct, more candid in introducing a novel, and it is a sign of the remarkable confidence that he now felt in his abilities that he was able to use a rhetoric so plain.

The feeling that *Jude* conveys is so direct and so powerful, that 'without a mincing of words' seems not an inappropriate description, but the structure which conveys that feeling is more carefully calculated than ever. Hardy, profiting from the experience of writing *The Well-Beloved* where he had made the symmetry of plot carry its own meaning, extends this in *Jude* so that the structure itself derives from that clash of contraries so basic to his imagination.

Of course the book is all contrasts – or was meant to be in its original conception. Alas, what a miserable accomplishment it is, when I compare it with what I meant to make it! – e.g. Sue and her heathen gods set against Jude's reading the Greek testament; Christminster academical, Christminster in the slums; Jude the saint, Jude the sinner; Sue the Pagan, Sue the saint; marriage, no marriage; etc. etc.[2]

Jude is the case of a novel not merely embodying a man's imagination, but miming the way it works. It is an index of how completely Hardy has come to know himself as an artist. This is not to say that *Jude* is an unequivocal success, but that by the time of *Jude* Hardy has assimilated his past as completely as a writer can and knows precisely what he can do. Or he almost does.

Father Time is the last, but in some ways the most dramatic, instance of Hardy continuing 'to feel for a method' in a novel where that whole notion had been ostentatiously put to one side. As a character Father Time marks the place where two kinds of fiction cross, in one he is 'Arabella's boy', in the other he is 'Age masquerading as Juvenility'. The crossing is an awkward one. But for our purpose, it is not the character, but the function of Father Time that matters. In Father Time Hardy was seeking to fill the gap created by the absence of Wessex, he needed the long perspective which reveals that while men may make their own plots, a plot may be made for them, the scenario of which can only be guessed at. Father Time was an actor in that script, forever old where Pierston was forever young. But Father Time has to carry more than his years, he is 'the expression in a single term' of the situation between Jude and Sue, and it is a function too great for him to bear. We sense the immensity of feeling behind his creation, but as an expression of those feelings, he is baffled, mute. Nevertheless, if we try to think of *Jude* without Father Time, it becomes a lesser novel, a tragedy not about the universe, but more about unfulfilled ambitions, domestic strife. Father Time marks the outermost reach of Hardy's art: the extravagance is too great – the stylisation fails; the formal and the realistic modes collide. But there is a sense in which the very violence of that collision is a measure of the author's creative energy, of his undiminished eagerness to encompass something new.

NOTES
1 F. E. Hardy, *The Life of Thomas Hardy*, Macmillan, 1962, p. 102.
2 Ibid., pp. 272–3.

10 How It Is for Thomas Hardy

Lance St. John Butler

We seem to be afraid of exercising in connection with literature the judgement that we exercise so freely in relation to life. We accept things from Dante and Herbert, from Dickens and Hafiz, that we would not take from our friends for a moment. We have developed a sort of doublethink whereby we somehow manage to avoid applying to literature the criteria we apply in every other sphere.

Thus, when Herbert or Hafiz addresses a Divine Being in whom we no longer believe, when Dante or Dickens proposes a cosmological order that is frankly ludicrous, we make allowances. Dante is a clear example of how this works. Mostly we think about his universe, and talk about it, as if it really existed. If we are jolted out of this and remember that his cosmology is in demonstrable error we easily fall back to the position that his poem is an allegory, and here we are happy to rest, thinking and talking allegorically. If we are then reminded that the allegory refers to a spiritual reality in which we have no faith we fall back on 'the writing' (or even 'the literature'), by which we mean Dante's language, his power to express his vision and his ability to create metaphor. In short, we make allowances for Dante's materialist cosmology, he knew no better perhaps, and we make allowances for his Christian world-view, comfortably accommodating it in spite of common sense.

Now I do not object to this process and I am not attempting the curious task of proving that Dante is bad, but I do think that we should be aware of this making of allowances and should try not to let it really become doublethink. The point is that 'making allowances' sorts ill with our professed regard for truth. When faced with Lear on the heath or Macbeth on the battlements we are very likely to insist, earnestly and even emotionally, that here we are in the presence of 'truth'. Human life, we imply, is truly the way Shakespeare depicts it : we do not have to say about him that he knew no better, we do not have to make allowances in his case.

Nobody, of course, supposes that this 'truth' of *Lear* and *Macbeth* is literal or historical truth, it obviously does not pass the verification test; but then art never is concerned with this sort of truth, indeed,

art *can* never be concerned with it. If the sculptor reproduces the
baked-bean tin perfectly he has created something more (and something less) than a tin of baked-beans. If a novelist were to indulge in
the Borgesian occupation of copying out a report from a newspaper
verbatim the result would be a different sort of thing from the
original report. Shakespeare, then, cannot be dealing with literal
truth, so we have to say that his truth is 'poetic' truth, and here's the
rub: we have no vocabulary to help us to distinguish between the
poetic truth of the *Inferno* and the poetic truth of *Lear*. We are
conveniently able to forget that they are true in different ways: the
Inferno is only perceived as true through the thick distorting mist of
all the allowances we have to make for Dante while *Lear* strikes us
as immediately and somehow 'really' true. The 'really' cannot mean
'literally' but must mean that the truth of *Lear* does not depend on a
distorted picture of the universe.

Shakespeare's picture of the universe is not distorted because,
finally, Shakespeare has no picture of the universe. By this I mean
that he has no given 'philosophy'. This is his great secret: 'a philosophy' is always wrong, a 'picture' always distorts. The universe is
inherently ambiguous, enigmatic and inexplicable: 'a philosophy'
cannot match this by definition. It is also true, however, that the
universe is richly and densely patterned. Shakespeare at his greatest
reflects this curious situation: the world is finally absurd, a tale told
by an idiot; but it is a tale, not a chaos; cause precedes effect and
men beget men and not pigs for all the ultimate meaninglessness of it.
As Conrad's Marlow has it, life is a 'mysterious arrangement of merciless logic for a futile purpose'.

This avoidance of a set *Weltanschauung* has been very rare in
literature.[1] It is obviously the most difficult position to adopt in an
art whose nature is expression and in a world where every expression
implies a theory and every theory points towards a certain cosmic
picture. I would like to claim, however, that this position was
sucessfully adopted by Hardy. To illustrate its rarity we can think
for a moment about two novelists who have very definite world-
views, George Eliot and Dickens.

Middlemarch is a great novel but it has the poetic truth of Dante,
not the poetic truth of Shakespeare. In its ending justice is done, the
good are rewarded and the bad punished. This is a distorted view of
reality; in truth there is no necessary connection between virtue and
happiness. We have to make allowances for George Eliot's belief that
there is such a connection or, at the least, we must make allowances
for her feeling that there should be such a connection. Either way
we are confronted with a fictional world distorted to conform to a
Providential cosmology. Hardy, like Shakespeare, presents a picture

of the world that does not conform to any predetermined cosmology, least of all a Providential one. I think it is important to recognise this distinction and to remember that we ourselves, if we conform at all to the broad trends of modern thought, probably do not see an ultimate Providential structure 'behind' the universe: should this not make some difference to our view of *Middlemarch*?

Similarly with Dickens. We no longer believe in the innocence of children, or in the sanctity of innocence, and perhaps this makes our admiration of Dickens somewhat inconsistent. We are sometimes embarrassed by his sentimentality but we rarely face the fact that this sentimentality is not simply an error of taste but the inevitable product of a world-view in which man comes into the world trailing clouds of glory. If we no longer possess that world-view should this not be taken into account in our estimate of Dickens?

Like Shakespeare, but unlike George Eliot and Dickens, Hardy had no 'philosophy'. On the other hand, Hardy's world, like Shakespeare's, is packed with considerations about life, death, man and the universe: neither writer, significantly, has much to say about God. This is not contradictory. Shakespeare and Hardy perceive the world to be richly and densely patterned and this patterning is the stuff of their art as it is of the art of others. But they also perceive no final cause, no meaning ultimately inhering in their patterns.[2] Neither writer remains for long in the rarified atmosphere of this perception. Shakespeare's comedies are often rather nearer to a Providential cosmology than his great tragedies are. Hardy's early novels imply a structured universe rather more than his later novels. But at their greatest they are able to abandon all support and face the truth.

Beckett, in the last of the *Three Dialogues with Georges Duthuit*, makes the following observation about creative artists:

> All have turned wisely tail, before the ultimate penury, back to the mere misery where destitute virtuous mothers may steal bread for their starving brats. There is more than a difference of degree between being short, short of the world, short of self, and being without these esteemed commodities. The one is a predicament, the other not.

Our doublethink lies between the two possibilities outlined in this. In our art and at our dinner-tables we proclaim loudly that the world *is* the ultimate penury, but we bracket this out when we read literature, especially the literature of the past. Without even noticing what we are doing we turn tail back to the destitute virtuous mothers and the predicament they present, quite forgetting that they depend on a world in which we do not believe.

Hardy speaks to us today, as Shakespeare does and Beckett does, because he faces the ultimate penury of the world. I would stress the word 'ultimate': the world is only *finally* empty, not immediately. On the immediate level there is the Forest of Arden, Talbothays Dairy, the bright whirl of the Unnamable's mind, the rich objective realities of human perception and experience. On the ultimate level, there is nothing.

A great deal of attention is paid by critics to the language and style of writers, to the formal aspects of literature. This emphasis seems to have caused a neglect of the more obvious aspect of any poem, play or novel: what it means. This 'what it means' I intend in the colloquial sense of a work's basic assumptions, its world-view, its overall purpose. Because of this neglect Hardy, a writer loved and admired by a far wider range of people than a good many novelists and poets exalted by the critical orthodoxy, has suffered absurdly. People are led to imagine that his supposed episodes of 'bad writing' automatically exclude him from the company of the great and no thought is given to the point that his world-view probably coincides far more closely with what we are now likely to see as the truth than the world-view of most of the said great.

It will, I am sure, be protested, it will have been protested long since, that Hardy, so far from having 'no philosophy', pictures the cosmos as completely structured and is, indeed, a notorious pessimist and determinist. But here we must try to be fair: the purpose of his structure is always to reveal the ultimate absence of structure. The whole purpose of *The Dynasts*, to take the most obvious example, is the construction of a supernatural scheme that will reveal that there is no supernatural scheme. I shall return to this point.

Meanwhile, to demonstrate my thesis in more detail, I shall consider the endings of Hardy's six major novels. At the end of a novel the writer inevitably shows his true colours: we have already glanced at the ending of *Middlemarch* and have seen that it falsifies reality in a way that we should at least recognise. We may enjoy it, approve it, be edified by it, but we must in all honesty reject it as a picture of the world. Mankind is not in the hands of Providence. Tertius Lydgate's suitable fate cannot have been planned for him as there is no Planner. By leaving him with the paltry achievement of a treatise on gout George Eliot is assuming a world in which achievement is linked to morality; such a world assumes a Providence and if we question *that* the whole structure crumbles and in its fall some damage must be done to our estimation of George Eliot. Hardy himself says of Newman's *Apologia* something similar to what I am saying about George Eliot. In the *Life* he quotes the following from his own notes:

> *July 2 (1865)* worked at J. H. Newman's *Apologia* . . . Style charming, and his logic really human, being based not on syllogisms but on converging probabilities. Only – and here comes the fatal catastrophe – there is no first link to his excellent chain of reasoning, and down you come headlong . . .

If we examine the endings of Hardy's six major novels we can see him struggling furiously in the marshes that separate the nineteenth century from the twentieth. Behind him are the illusory certainties of the old world, before him the wasteland of the new. He belongs to both worlds and to neither.[3]

At the end of *Far from the Madding Crowd* Hardy finds a solution that seems like a compromise. Troy and Boldwood go into the darkness and, at long last and in a very muted key, the humble hero gets the part-worn reward of the heroine's hand. Hardy obviously feels that he needs to justify even this limited 'happy ending' and he does so by claiming that Oak and Bathsheba can hope for some happiness because there is a sort of love, bred of working side-by-side, that is stronger than mere volatile passion. This claim is unsatisfactory in two ways. First, the novel is clearly about passionate love; Oak and Bathsheba are not just two old companions who eventually decide to marry. Second, Hardy's claim reinforces the moral aspect of the novel: Oak has *deserved* Bathsheba, he has patiently served his apprenticeship, like Hercules for Omphale, and he *merits* the reward he gets. There is still the skeleton of a moral and Providential structure behind this novel.

The *Return of the Native* is more complex. The heath destroys the passionate aspirations of the most unstable characters, Wildeve and Eustacia, by destroying the characters themselves. Perhaps this can be read as a moral (nature destroys those who do not care about her) but if so it is an ambiguous moral, for Mrs Yeobright, too, is destroyed by the heath. Clym wanders out of the novel an unresolved character, which is promising, although he does achieve some degree of self-knowledge and fulfilment. Diggory Venn and Thomasin, on the other hand, in coming to marriage and prosperity, show Hardy throwing in his hand and opting for the old-world, Providential solution. In this context it is highly significant that Hardy saw fit to include in the definitive edition of this novel a note to the effect that he would have preferred a different ending, one in which Venn would have departed into the heath, mysterious and unresolved.

By the time Hardy wrote *The Mayor of Casterbridge* his need for the conventional Providential scheme had begun to break up seriously. Farfrae gets Lucetta, and later Elizabeth-Jane, by the casual chances of life; Newson appears casually and casually takes a happiness of which we cannot say that he did or did not deserve it; Henchard suffers and suffers, and finally dies with his suffering unresolved. His agony brings him nothing and avails him nothing.

In *The Woodlanders* Fitzpiers is reunited with Grace at the end because he takes rational action to win her back, not because he deserves her. Taking his fate into his own hands he tries to attract her again and he succeeds. We are specifically told that a good deal of his success is due to Grace's own restlessness and the passage of time. Marty South suffers over Giles dead as she suffered over him living. Worthy as she is and suffering as she does there is no reward for her except the reward of memory.

In *Tess of the d'Urbervilles* the 'pure woman' is not rewarded for her purity. The casual fate that brings her Alec also brings her Angel, alas in that order. It could easily have been otherwise if Tess had danced with Angel at the club walking day at Marlott but it is as it is and all the ensuing suffering brings her only to an ignoble death. For the gods Tess is only 'sport' (a perfect absurdist image for the contingency of existence). The discomfort we feel at the sudden introduction of 'Liza-'Lu at the end, as Angel's reward, proves the point I am making: by the time of *Tess* we expect something truer from Hardy than this sort of Providential ending and, not surprisingly, the critical consensus is that 'Liza-'Lu's rôle at the end of the novel is an inconsistency.

With *Jude the Obscure* Hardy finally achieves his goal of writing a novel with an ending that is not false and he needs to go no further. It may seem ironic that in order to do this he has to manipulate and control events to an almost bizarre extent.[4] After all, have we not questioned the way in which George Eliot controls the ending of *Middlemarch* with false laws? But, of course, I am not at all saying that an artist should not control his material: to be an artist *is* to control your material, to rework it into new patterns and significant orders. My point is that we do not sufficiently distinguish between those writers who order their material according to a blueprint which is, alas, false and those other writers who order their material to reflect the lack of a final blueprint.

Thus, in *Jude the Obscure* the ending gives nobody what they deserve. We feel no satisfaction in the contemplation of Jude's fate or Sue's or Phillotson's or Arabella's. Jude deserved better at the hands of the world although much of his suffering was of his own making. Sue is the victim of her own psychology, of society, of the random and hideous fact of the deaths of her children; again, some of her fate is of her own choosing. Phillotson has a moment of generosity which costs him his wife and his job. Towards the end of the novel he acts rather less generously and it gets him back a travesty of a wife but not his job. So the world goes: there *are* causes and effects, Hardy is a master at constructing intricate chains of them, but they do not rely in any way on moral or supernatural considerations. Arabella is normally selfish and always vulgar and yet she survives reasonably well, not least because she is able to take her life into her own hands to some extent without feeling hampered by moral considerations. Her survival depends on her ability to read the world correctly and her reading of it is clearly that it is not a moral structure. She perceives without effort how the world works and in doing so reveals that it does not work according to Providential ordinance.

So, by the time of *Jude the Obscure*, Hardy has struggled out of the marshland and has finally found his footing on the inhospitable soil of modern thought.

Those who feel that the absurdist view of the world is inaccurate will naturally object to my using that view as synonymous with 'the truth'. My point, however, still largely holds even if the absurdist view is rejected. Firstly it is still legitimate to suggest that we should pay some attention to the different world-views of different writers: whatever our own views may be we should still notice the difference between the cosmologies underlying works of art in our estimate of them. Secondly, even if we are not absurdists we may not be Christians, in which case the problem of Dante and Dickens remains. Thirdly there is the matter, already raised, of Hardy's 'philosophy': like Shakespeare, Hardy has no 'philosophy' except in the negative sense in which having no philosophy is itself a philosophy. This is the sense, too, in which absurdism is a philosophy and we must not forget that it *is* negative: when we talk of Hardy's philosophy or of absurdism we are employing a kind of shorthand which signifies a view of the world which has sloughed off the dubious consolation of Divine Order or Ultimate Meaning, that is all. Hardy expresses the 'real truth' simply in so far as he does not resort to the 'truths' that sustain, for example, Christian or Marxist literature. Only if we are believers of the Christian or Marxist sort will we want seriously to challenge his *Weltanschauung*.

All that I have said so far relies on the assumption that Hardy rejects any final order in the universe. What, then, of the various sorts of order that appear so clearly in his work? Is he not guilty of imposing his own version of cosmic order on his plots? Is he not also, notoriously, given to employing fatalistic and deterministic devices and, further, to giving capital letters to expressions such as Immanent Will and Unfulfilled Intention?

I shall deal with these questions under two heads: fatalism, and the Immanent Will. First, then, does Hardy employ a cosmic order when he introduces patterns of fatalism into his plots? In *Jude the Obscure*, for instance, there is the matter of the doom that seems to hang over the family to which Jude and Sue belong: old Miss Fawley and widow Edlin wag their heads ominously and observe that Jude's family is fated not to marry well, that marriage, especially to a cousin, will bring disaster. What are we to make of this? Or what are we to make of Henchard's ruin? Is he not like Job? Does he not appear to be a scapegoat, a victim of divine wrath? Is it not as though some fate, predetermined and inescapable, is pursuing him?

I would claim that this sort of determinism in Hardy is only apparent and that he indulges in it for artistic reasons while making quite sure that we do not take it literally. First of all he always provides us with adequate reasons for all his characters' actions so that we do not have to resort to believing his fatalistic asides. He offers plenty of perfectly natural explanations of the causes of Jude's tragedy and Henchard's. Jude's impractical dreaminess, his romantic but sexually alive temperament and his tolerance, together with Sue's neurasthenic insecurity and the hostile social environment in which they both live quickly add up to a sufficient reason for the failure of their marriage. We do not need to resort to gloomy prophecies about their ancestry; Hardy includes the fatalistic theme of their heredity as a device to set the tone, to keep before us the despair-filled background to their love, not to explain it. Similarly with Henchard. His ruin is brought about by his headstrong temperament, by his impatience with detail, by his passionate response to the world and, of course, by bad weather and bad luck. Most importantly, for my purposes, his ruin is in part brought about by his visit to the weather-prophet; here, if anywhere, Hardy is pointing out that there is no supernatural order to which man can appeal: weather will go on being weather and conform to its own laws for all the prayers and prophecies man can devise. So, far from being fated to fail by the gods, Henchard is ruined by himself and by the chances of life; there is the ironic twist, even, that he is ruined by believing in the supernatural.

This is how Hardy's 'philosophy' always works. Any apparent intervention by fate, destiny or some other external determinism, however freely Hardy employs it for artistic reasons, is overwhelmed, in the end, by the provision of a heap of circumstances that adequately explain the apparently fated events. In the end the super-

F

natural point of view is relegated to the status of the story of the d'Urberville coach in *Tess*: a vague dark presence vestigially present behind the story, explaining nothing.

Our second question concerned the expressions 'the Immanent Will' and 'the Unfulfilled Intention'. If Hardy really eschews philosophical systems and progressively abandons the method of writing novels that tacitly accepts a meaningful world-order, where do these famous expressions come from with their capital letters and their air of self-assured metaphysics?

The answer lies in the fact that these concepts are only intended metaphorically, as a moment's thought about them will reveal. The Immanent Will *is immanent*. That is to say it is not transcendent, not external to the world, not supernatural. It *is* the world, it is the sum total of all the motion and motivation that 'makes the world go round'. Instead of the echoing silence of a universal *stasis* the cosmos is in frantic motion. Galaxies revolve and blood sings along arteries. By analogy with man, for whom motion presupposes motive, Hardy implies a motive, a will, generating this cosmic activity. But only by analogy. What he is searching for is an expression that will denote the inherent dynamism of the universe *without* importing religious or supernatural connotations. His problem is that of the biologist who needs to introduce an expression such as 'natural selection': the words half-imply a supernatural agent (a Will, Nature, a Selector) but this implication is not intended. Hardy makes himself perfectly clear on this in the discussion that opens *The Dynasts*. In the first line of the Fore Scene the Shade of the Earth asks:

What of the Immanent Will and Its designs?

The Spirit of the Years replies:

> It works unconsciously, as heretofore,
> Eternal artistries in Circumstance,
> Whose patterns, wrought by rapt aesthetic rote,
> Seem in themselves Its single listless aim,
> And not their consequence.

In the ensuing exchanges the Spirit of the Years observes that some have claimed that the Will has grown tired of Earth and now ignores it, others that early man was deservedly deserted by God (the reference is unambiguously Christian). These opinions the Spirit of the Years rejects. Then the Spirit of the Pities asks whether the Immanent Will might not awaken at some future date. The Spirit of the Years answers:

Nay. In the Foretime, even to the germ of Being,
Nothing appears of shape to indicate
That cognizance has marshalled things terrene,
Or will (such is my thinking) in my span.
Rather they show that, like a knitter drowsed,
Whose fingers play in skilled unmindfulness,
The Will has woven with an absent heed
Since life first was; and ever will so weave.

What order, then, is there for Hardy to impose on his fictions? They are, after all, well-orchestrated and minutely planned. The answer must simply be that he imposes an order that *is* an order but that implies that there is no final order. The image of the 'skilled unmind-fulness' of the drowsy knitter is as close as the human mind can come to understanding the paradox that, in this richly-patterned universe, there is no ultimate meaning. Whatever happens in Hardy's major fiction, however much he manipulates and controls it, he finally finds out how to prevent it from falling into a contrived moral or supernatural order. The novels from *Far from the Madding Crowd* to *Jude the Obscure* represent a resolute attempt to write fiction based on a view of things not as they might be in fantasy, nor as they can seem when we have made enough allowances, but as they are.

NOTES

1 I am aware that, formally, the view I ascribe to Shakespeare here is as much a *Weltanschauung*, as much philosophical, as Dante's. But this formal objection is pedantic: there is a difference between having 'a philosophy' and having the philosophy that no 'philosophy' works.

2 Hardy's success in expressing his perception, like Shakespeare's and Beckett's, shows where Robbe-Grillet goes wrong in *Pour un nouveau roman* when he calls for the elimination of *all* meaning from the novel. With Gallic radicalism he maintains that if the universe is meaningless then the art that reflects it should be meaningless too. He ignores the paradox that although the universe is absurd it is so only formally, in the sense that it lacks a final cause; it is not absurd in the sense of being a chaotic jumble, as the capacity of M. Robbe-Grillet to write coherent French proves.

3 Both: his 'churchiness' is old-world, his agnosticism new. Neither: compare the poems inspired by Emma's death in his *Poems 1912–13* with, on the one hand, *In Memoriam* and, on the other, Sylvia Plath. Hardy has a tone different from either of these.

4 Hardy was aware of what he was doing and in the *Life* called Jude a 'puppet'.

11 Thomas Hardy: The Man in his Work

F. E. Halliday

When I was reading English at Cambridge in the 1920s our literature appeared to finish with Queen Victoria; at least, as far as I remember, the work of no living writer formed part of the syllabus. Hardy, therefore, was my own discovery, and I vividly remember that January morning of 1928 when I opened the paper and read of his death. By 1930 I had read all his works and, with the help of Hermann Lea's *Thomas Hardy's Wessex*, explored much of Dorset, visited St Juliot, and in the autumn of that year had tea with Mrs Hardy at Max Gate. Shortly afterwards I read a paper on Hardy to a literary society, and I think somewhat astonished my audience by maintaining that his poetry was even more important than his novels, though a young poet sitting beside me, Cecil Day-Lewis, agreed.

I mention these things to show how much Hardy meant to me fifty years ago, and to suggest how much he still means, not only because he was a great writer but also because he was a great and lovable man. One approach, therefore, to an appreciation of Hardy today is to trace the revelation of the man in his work in the course of his long life. This divides itself quite naturally into three almost equal periods of thirty years, each broken in the middle by some decisive event.

First, 1840–70. The eldest of four children, he was born in a cottage at Bockhampton on the edge of Egdon Heath about two miles east of Dorchester, of humble parents, his father being a builder who played the fiddle in the choir of the neighbouring church of Stinsford, as well as at local junketings. His mother, a devout intelligent woman, encouraged the boy's reading, and her fatalistic view of life must have been partly responsible for his interest in the grotesque and macabre. Music, dancing, books and the Church. He left school at sixteen in the early days of penny post and railway, and it is important to realise that during those formative years life for him was concentrated within the few square miles between Egdon, Stinsford and the little country town of Dorchester. Even the next five years were spent there as apprentice to a Dorchester architect, though his horizon was widened by a friendly young Cambridge man, Horace Moule, who acted almost as a private tutor. He was twenty-one when he first left home to become an architect's assistant in London, yet after five years he returned to help first a Dorchester, then a Weymouth architect. And shortly after his return he fell in love with his young cousin Tryphena Sparks.

One of Hardy most attractive qualities was his modesty, his lack of worldly ambition. Like Jude Fawley he had not wanted to grow up, and in later life felt he would rather have been a cathedral organist than anything. When in London he thought of entering the Church so that he could find time for writing poetry, though we can understand why he abandoned this idea if we read one of the poems, 'Hap', that he wrote at this time when the works of Comte, Mill, Darwin, Huxley and Swinburne were shaping his philosophy. All his poems were rejected by the impercipient Victorian editors, and on his return to Bockhampton he turned to prose and wrote a novel, *The Poor Man and the Lady*.

Hardy was to maintain that there was more autobiography in a hundred lines of his poetry than in all his novels. This was the attempt of a shy and sensitive man to deceive would-be biographers, and he himself wrote the story of his life, or what he chose to reveal, which was to be published after his death as having been written by his wife. It is true that it was chiefly in his poetry that Hardy revealed his inner spiritual life, and this is the main reason why his poetry is so moving, but it is also true that in some of his novels, particularly his early and inferior ones, he revealed, thinly disguised, many more mundane happenings. Thus, though *The Poor Man* was never published and the manuscript destroyed, we know that the poor man lived in the Hardy cottage, became assistant to a London architect and, like Hardy, won a prize for an architectural essay. Incidentally, it contained the first of his melodramatic night-scenes in a church, presumably Stinsford. Hardy the agnostic was 'churchy', as he put it, in more senses than one. He was also a romantic: a Victorian gothic architect delighting in medieval irregularity and grotesquery rather than in classical balance and serenity.

The Poor Man was another failure, but it served as a quarry for later novels, as did his unpublished poems, and he tried again, and wrote the gothically sensational *Desperate Remedies*. The pattern repeated itself. The scene centres on Stinsford church and neighbouring Kingston Maurward House where a childless lady had almost adopted him when he was a small boy attending the school she had built. And again the hero is a poor man, assistant to an architect in

Weymouth where, as Hardy rowed Tryphena, he rowed a young lady about the bay before going to London to further his profession. Well-read in Shakespeare, he is himself a poet in a small way until he decides that writing verse ruins a man for any useful occupation. Then the villain takes over and melodramatic fiction begins. Hardy had almost finished the novel when he was asked by his employer to go to St Juliot near Tintagel to take measurements of the church he was to restore there. So early in the morning of 7 March 1870 he set out for Lyonnesse, and that evening met the fair-haired, blue-eyed sister-in-law of the rector, Emma Gifford. It was the end of the first thirty-year period of his life.

At this time he had published nothing, but the second period, 1870–97, was to see the appearance of fourteen novels as well as three volumes of short stories. *Desperate Remedies*, 1871, was followed a year later by *Under the Greenwood Tree*, an expansion of the first chapters of *The Poor Man*, the scene little more than the area between the Hardy cottage and Stinsford, speech an affectionately humorous version of that of Dorset rustics. Though it is not strictly autobiographical, for the action is supposed to take place shortly before Hardy's birth, some of the characters are portraits, and Tranter Reuben, owner of the cottage and fiddle-player in the church, is obviously very like Hardy's genial easy-going father. And the dark-haired dark-eyed Fancy Day who becomes mistress of the Stinsford school at Christmas strongly resembles, at least in appearance, Tryphena Sparks, who became headmistress of a Plymouth school at Christmas 1871. But Tryphena was very different from Elfride Swancourt, the fair-haired heroine of his next novel; for Hardy had revisited St Juliot and written *A Pair of Blue Eyes*, in which he described these early meetings very much as he was to describe them fifty years later in his autobiography. Although Elfride and Stephen Smith are ten years younger than Emma and Hardy, she is daughter of a vicar on the north Cornish coast, and he a humbly-born assistant architect who has come to make plans for the restoration of the church. The evening drive from Launceston to St Juliot is described, as are the meeting with Emma and expeditions along the coast, she riding her mare, he walking beside her. Autobiography could go no further at this early stage of their romance, and after the opening chapters fact inevitably fades into fantasy, with a humorous chorus of Dorset, not Cornish, rustics. Yet there is one memorable scene of self-revelation: the thoughts of Knight as he clings to a cliff and finds himself gazing at a trilobite, 'face to face with the beginning and all the intermediate centuries simultaneously'. Victorians did not believe in such things, but here is the essential Hardy, for whom the present was ever a re-entry into the past.

The year 1874 was a memorable one, for, after serialisation, *Far from the Madding Crowd* was published, first of his great 'Novels of Character and Environment'. There is little obvious autobiography, but Hardy is a constant presence, guide to the scene near his home and interpreter of the first two great characters of his creation, Gabriel Oak and Bathsheba Everdene. The novel was a great success, so, abandoning Tryphena as well as the profession of architect, he married Emma and began his career as professional novelist.

It began badly, for Emma, having escaped from Cornwall, had no intention of being stranded in Dorset, so they took rooms in London where Hardy began *The Hand of Ethelberta* to show that his gifts as a novelist were not confined to rural life in Wessex. Yet they were, or rather, his genius was. However, the book finished with scenes in east Dorset, near Swanage, to which the couple moved before settling for two years at Sturminster Newton in north Dorset. There Hardy wrote his second great novel, *The Return of the Native*, so appropriately named even though he had not yet quite returned to his native scene. In later life he was to write of his hero Clym Yeobright, 'I think he is the nicest of my heroes, and *not a bit* like me.' Which means, of course, that he is. For the unambitious solitude-loving Clym is almost a self-portrait: a man in whom natural cheerfulness strives against depression from without; who has reached the stage when the grimness of the human situation has become clear. Egdon itself, 'slighted and enduring', symbolises the predicament of man, and the book ends with Hardy's first reference to a First Cause for whose oppression man has to invent excuses.

After what were, for Hardy at least, two idyllic years at Sturminster, the Dorset native returned to London, no doubt at Emma's insistence, and there, he was to note, 'their troubles began'. However, it was there that he wrote *The Trumpet-Major*, a romance of south Dorset during the Napoleonic Wars. But its successor, *A Laodicean*, was a disaster. It begins with autobiography in the manner of *Desperate Remedies*. The hero is a young architect who, after two years of writing verse and thoughts of entering the Church, resumes his profession, hears music that reminds him of the old west-gallery days, and argues about infant baptism as Hardy himself had argued twenty years before. The story then plunges into the melodrama of his first novel eked out with padding. But Hardy was a sick man when he wrote, or rather dictated, most of the book while lying prostrate in bed.

London, he at last realised, was bad not only for his health but also for his profession; Dorset was the source of his inspiration, and soon after his recovery in 1881 he returned for good. He made a concession to Emma, however: they would go to London each year for 'the season'. So he rented a house in Wimborne, again only just across the border, and there wrote *Two on a Tower*, a romance about astronomy, a subject that fascinated him, though a poet's conception of the infinite grandeur of the universe did not encourage conventional views about its origin.

Then, after two years in Wimborne, the native really returned, when in 1883 he rented a house in Dorchester, and there wrote the first of his sequence of four great tragic novels, *The Mayor of Casterbridge*. The scene is the Dorchester of his early schooldays, when he walked up the High Street where tethered horses with forefeet on the pavement nipped him as he passed, and the two worn bridges at the bottom were peopled by men whose dust mingled with that of imperial Rome. Hardy rarely intrudes – though the last paragraph is revealing – but he is always there, an unseen presence in this novel without a heroine, but with a hero whose fate is tragic as that of Lear whom in so many ways he resembles.

While writing the novel Hardy had been building a house just outside Dorchester. He and Emma had been married for ten years yet had never had a house of their own, and 'the worst of taking a furnished house is that the articles in the rooms are saturated with the thoughts and glances of others.' In the summer of 1885, therefore – marking the middle of Hardy's life – they moved into Max Gate, where he wrote *The Woodlanders*. 'As a story' he liked it best of his novels, partly because of the scene, which was the Blackmore Vale of apple-orchards; yet, although he could describe, or rather interpret, a scene in prose much as Turner could interpret in paint, beauty of appearance meant little without beauty of association, the presence of a human figure, and 'mountains are unimportant beside the wear on a threshold'. The story he so much liked, therefore, was that of Giles Winterborne, another very human figure, yet almost legendary, almost the personification of Autumn.

Tess followed, this time a novel without a hero – for there is nothing heroic about the prig of a husband who abandons her – but with a heroine on the scale of Henchard. All Hardy's compassion went into the making of Tess, 'a pure woman', who weeps as she puts an end to the agony of birds wounded by sportsmen, and kills the man who has wronged her to show how much she loves her repentant husband. And again, in the last paragraph Hardy himself speaks : 'The President of the Immortals, in Aeschylean phrase, had finished his sport with Tess.' But a sadistic tyrant was not his final conception of the President.

By the time he wrote *Tess* his relations with Emma had completely broken down. The twentieth anniversary of their first meeting was on 7 March 1890 and, ironically enough, it was now that he heard of the death of Tryphena, the cousin he might have married had he not gone to St Juliot. He had been thinking about her and now wrote 'Thoughts of Phena', a poem of grief and regret for his 'lost prize'. Then, shortly after publication of *Tess*, he wrote the serial story *The Pursuit of the Well-Beloved*, the essence of which is scarcely-veiled autobiography, though nobody was to know it at the time. A young Dorset sculptor, instead of marrying his young cousin, marries a lady with whom he quarrels, then twenty years later he hears that his cousin is dead. Although he had left her because his feeling had been one of friendship rather than love, he now 'loved the woman dead as he had never loved her in life', and youthful friendship 'flamed into a passionate attachment, embittered by regret beyond words'. It is Hardy speaking, haunter and idealiser of the past. Another twenty years and he was to mourn another woman dead, whom he had long ceased to love when alive. Meanwhile he began to write *Jude the Obscure*.

Hardy maintained that of all his novels *Jude* had least to do with his own life; which means that it had most. There is autobiography in the early years of Jude, who comes from Mellstock (Stinsford), and there is more of the inner life of Hardy in the book than in all the other novels put together. It is essentially an attack on hypocritical Victorian insistence on conformity, particularly on its laws governing marriage. 'The letter killeth' says the epigraph on the title-page, and, having broken the non-conforming Sue, it kills the non-conforming Jude. And Hardy as Chorus: 'the First Cause worked automatically like a somnambulist', without a thought of the sentient human beings who were to develop on this earth. It was prologue to *The Dynasts*.

That work, however, had to wait a few years. *Jude* was published late in 1895, despite Emma's attempts to prevent it, and after writing a revised and unimproved version of *The Well-Beloved*, which appeared in 1897, Hardy turned with relief to his first love, verse, in which he felt he could say things unacceptable in prose. It was the end of the second period of his life, and in 1898 he began the third and last with the publication of *Wessex Poems*.

In his Preface he wrote, and was often to repeat, that many of his poems were dramatic even when not obviously so. Maybe: yet many of his poems were personal even when professedly dramatic, for he agreed with Leslie Stephen that 'the ultimate aim of a poet should be to touch our hearts by showing his own'. And no other poet has shown so much of his own as Hardy, and it is the revelation of this shy, troubled, generous, compassionate heart that makes his poetry so endearing and, at its best, so great. Like his novels, his poems are about people, though not only about people living, but people dead,

F*

and 'people' and 'memories' are almost the keywords to his poetry. Thus, in 'Friends Beyond' he celebrated the Mellstock Quire and others who then lay in the churchyard, and an 1870 lyric to Emma was followed by thoughts of the phantom Phena in 1890. Then, in 'The Impercipient' the reluctant agnostic asked why he could not share the faith of others, and he wondered if some Automaton had shaped the world and its suffering creatures. Prelude again to *The Dynasts*, as were the poems about the Napoleonic Wars. But in 1899 another war began, in South Africa, and in one of his finest lyrics, 'The Darkling Thrush', written on the last evening of the century, Hardy wondered if the frail bird's ecstatic song was one of hope for something of which he was unaware.

Poems of the Past and the Present followed in 1901. Of the past was 'The Self-Unseeing', an unforgettable autobiographical lyric of his dancing as a child to his father's fiddle while his mother smiled into the fire, all three unconscious of their happiness. Of the present there were war poems, not of patriotism but pity, and he thought of how the body of a Wessex drummer would grow into some African tree, as flowers growing in Stinsford churchyard were once Fanny Hurd and others buried there. Always people in things, and even Shelley's skylark might still be throbbing in some Italian myrtle. But if Hardy always saw the past in the present, was so full of memories, the 'Lord Most High' whom he visited in a dream-poem had quite forgotten his insignificant creation of earth and the human race.

But the Immanent Will of *The Dynasts* had not forgotten, for It had never remembered, never known what It had done. Much of Hardy's life had been a preparation for the writing of this epic-drama of the last ten years of the Napoleonic Wars : his grandfather had been in the Home Guard of the period, his grandmother had told him tales of those times, and some of his earliest reading had been about them; Egdon Heath was full of relics, and Nelson's Hardy almost a neighbour; he had visited Waterloo and other scenes, and in *The Trumpet-Major* written about the Wessex of those days. Yet, great and original work though *The Dynasts* is, the scene is too distant, too vast, the action too remote to reveal much of the life of its Wessex author. Napoleon is no Henchard, there is no Tess, and very little of the Dorset countryside; and the blank verse, a new medium for Hardy, is oddly monotonous for a man who admired irregularity. The most memorable scenes are those of humble prose-speakers : Private Cantle on Egdon, the Wessex sailors who 'broached the Adm'l', the English deserters and their dying women. It is true that Hardy speaks at least once as Chorus of the Years in the characteristic lines describing the terrified small animals at Waterloo, and always as Chorus of the

Pities. Yet he finishes on a false, or forced, note: that the Will is becoming conscious and will 'fashion all things fair'.

That is very different from 'A Plaint to Man', written shortly afterwards. The fading phasm created by man tells him that the fact must be faced,

> The fact of life with dependence placed
> On the human heart's resource alone,
> In brotherhood bonded close and graced
> With loving-kindness fully blown,
> And visioned help unsought, unknown.

Man, not a man-created god, is responsible for man. It is a summary of his mature philosophy.

The poem was published in *Satires of Circumstance*, the title of which may account for the juxtaposition of two love-poems: 'When I set out for Lyonnesse', celebrating his first meeting with Emma, and 'A Thunderstorm in Town', a recent parting from another woman. Then suddenly, in November 1912, Emma died. Filled with memories and remorse, exactly forty-three years after their first meeting, he re-entered the past and her olden haunts at St Juliot. 'He loved the woman dead' as he had not loved her since their early days together, and to the young woman of forty years before he wrote some of the greatest love-poems ever written:

> O the opal and the sapphire of that wandering western sea,
> And the woman riding high above with bright hair flapping free –
> The woman whom I loved so, and who loyally loved me.

A year later the childless man of nearly seventy-four married Florence Dugdale, a woman young enough to have been his daughter, so that the last half of the last period of his life was one of serenity at Max Gate. And the poems continued to flow. First, the war poems: 'The Pity of It', that English and Germans, so closely related, should be fighting one another, and a dream-poem in which he finds that there are no foreigners, that his country is the world. And as well as for men and women there are poems of compassion and pleading for all living things, for trees, birds and animals, as he thought of himself as one of whom they were not afraid, and wondered if he would be remembered as one who used to notice such things. Then there are poems about man-made things, both romantic and prosaic, things that evoke memories and thoughts of people: old furniture, the skeleton of a sunshade, a second-hand suit, and always there are thoughts of the early Emma, sometimes at St Juliot, sometimes at

Sturminster where she had once waited for him 'with high-expectant heart'. And so to the triumphant 'Ancient to Ancients' and last words to the World that had never promised more than it had given.

But what other writer has given more to the world than the generous, compassionate Thomas Hardy? No other English-writing novelist has created characters on the heroic scale of Henchard and Tess, and so recreated their environment; no playwright has written a drama on the epic scale of *The Dynasts*, and no other poet has so endearingly revealed his heart. This does not mean that Hardy is the equal of Shakespeare, but it does mean that he is one of those who most nearly rival him, like Chaucer, with whom he has so much in common. Then, Hardy was among the leaders of thought in his age, a meliorist who realised the potential grandeur of man, yet one driven almost to despair by the slowness of his progress. In *Jude*, written twenty years before the first World War, he had asked, 'When people of a later age look back upon the barbarous customs and superstitions of the times that we have the unhappiness to live in, what *will* they say?' What, one wonders, would he say of the times we live in nearly a century later? But then, as he wrote in one of his loveliest lyrics, 'I shall mind not, slumbering peacefully.'

In 1916 he had been asked to contribute a poem to the Shakespeare celebrations of that year, and characteristically wrote of Stratford neighbours listening to the poet's passing-bell in 1616:

> – 'Ah, one of the tradesmen's sons, I now recall . . .
>   Witty, I've heard . . .
> We did not know him . . . Well, good-day. Death comes to all.'

Death came to Hardy twelve years later, and now after another fifty years we remember with affection and gratitude another tradesman's son, witty and, like Shakespeare, a lover of humanity.

12 Thomas Hardy: Fifty Years of Textual Scholarship

R. C. Schweik

Over the last fifty years, studies of Hardy published by some of the most talented literary historians and critics have been compromised because they were based on radically defective editions and written without full information about the development of Hardy's texts. The work of J. W. Beach is an early and particularly ironic case in point. By 1922 Beach had already published a pioneering study (*PMLA*, 1921) which documented the existence of bowdlerised versions of Hardy's writings; he had also helped Mary Ellen Chase prepare a fuller study of similar textual variants for the 1922 doctoral thesis she later published as *Thomas Hardy: From Serial to Novel* (1927). Although these early studies were conducted in ignorance both of manuscript evidences and of great differences between the Macmillan 1912 'Wessex' edition and some American editions, nevertheless they clearly demonstrated the need to be alert to possibly significant variants in Hardy's texts. Yet, when Beach prepared his own critical study, *The Technique of Thomas Hardy* (1922), he chose to use not the available 'Wessex' edition but, rather, a Harper printing that included a text of *The Woodlanders* which incorporated none of the revisions Hardy had made after 1887 and which, in fact, exhibited precisely the kinds of bowdlerising that Beach himself had previously deplored.

More recent literary historians and critics have sometimes fared as badly: Albert J. Guerard, for example, whose *Thomas Hardy: The Novels and Stories* (1949) was the first major reassessment of Hardy's achievement from a distinctly modern point of view, depended upon an edition so defective that more than a dozen of the illustrative quotations he used contained substantive variations from the 'Wessex' text, and doubtless thousands of others played a part in shaping his judgements; similarly, in *The English Novel: Form and Function* (1953), Dorothy Van Ghent lavished her splendid sensitivity to verbal nuance on a text of *Tess of the d'Urbervilles* that was at a far remove from Hardy's final intention. H. M. Reichard (*Explicator*, 1956) has noted one consequence of such carelessness: he points out that both Guerard and Van Ghent put great interpretative emphasis on a passage in which they assumed Hardy was referring to Tess and other milk-maids when, in fact, the wording of the 'Wessex' edition makes clear Hardy was actually describing cows!

Nor is the critic's or literary historian's problem simply one of using the best currently available text of Hardy's works: informed scholarship depends, too, upon knowledge of the textual history of those works, and when that information is not available, misinter-pretation is likely to result. Thus, in a discussion of Hardy's use of symbolic settings in *Far from the Madding Crowd*, Howard Babb (*ELH*, 1963) described the swamp near which Bathsheba sleeps as a 'symbol of her earlier despair' and concluded that 'the frightfully dark colours with which Hardy paints the swamp' were 'determined largely by its . . . symbolism'. Unless he had minutely examined some eleven leaves of a cancelled first-draft chapter of *Far from the Madding Crowd* now in the Dorset County Museum, Professor Babb could hardly have known that the 'colours' of the swamp were in fact originally chosen by Hardy as background for a completely different scene with entirely different emotional overtones. Nearly ten years would pass before R. C. Schweik (*English Studies*, 1972) would call attention to the bearing of Hardy's self-borrowing on Babb's inter-pretation, and there is still no edition of *Far from the Madding Crowd* which provides the critic with such textual information.

The fact is that in the fifty years since the death of Thomas Hardy no really coordinated effort has been made to provide the scholarly critical editions which the aesthetic value of his work warrants and which a fully informed literary criticism requires. What scholarship does exist on Hardy's texts has largely been the result of efforts by individual scholars, sometimes brilliant and substantial, often weak and disappointing, and all of it, in a very real sense, only preparatory to the publication of the kind of authoritative critical editions, com-plete with definitive apparatus, which are the final goal of modern textual scholarship. It is my purpose here to trace the developments which brought us to this state in the history of scholarship on Hardy's texts. Unfortunately, limitations of space make it impossible to touch on every relevant work: there are, for example, some unpublished dissertations which I must overlook and, to take a very different instance, there are a host of small notes on Hardy texts published by the indefatigable Carl Weber, many of which cannot be mentioned here. However, I do hope to provide a relatively full account of the development of textual scholarship on Hardy and to point towards what major work remains to be done. In doing so it will be useful to distinguish between three different though closely related areas of study: descriptive bibliography, textual analysis, and editing.

DESCRIPTIVE BIBLIOGRAPHY

The preliminary task of textual scholarship – the identification and description of a writer's manuscripts and printed texts – began with descriptive bibliographies by Henry Danielson (1916), A. P. Webb (1916), and John Lane (1894; revised 1923) – all seriously incomplete and intended primarily for collectors of first editions. Not until the publication of Richard L. Purdy's *Thomas Hardy: A Bibliographical Study* (1954; reprinted 1968) did scholars finally have a really comprehensive and highly reliable descriptive bibliography, a model of patient accuracy and thoroughness which remains today the best available single source of information on Hardy's manuscripts and the evolution of his texts. The 1968 reprinting of Purdy's book included some very important changes – such as a correction of his erroneous statement that the Mellstock edition had been printed from the same plates as the Wessex – but these constituted nothing like a full revision, and the 1968 version retains, therefore, most of the strengths and weaknesses of the 1954 original – e.g., it provides detailed collations, elaborately full information on bindings, and a truly extraordinary amount of detail about the texts and the circumstances of their composition and publication, but it says scarcely anything about typefaces, type sizes, text dimensions, and kinds of paper, nor does it usually provide full information about such matters as the number and location of copies examined. And, of course, it was prepared without the advantage of considering some valuable proposals published in the last ten years for practices which would give much greater precision to bibliographic descriptions of cloth patterns, binding colours, paper types and sizes, typography, and the like. Inevitably, too, research has thrown new light on Hardy's texts, sometimes in ways so dramatic as Dale Kramer's discovery of two important variant texts of *The Woodlanders* (*Studies in Bibliography*, 1967), but more often by the publication of little-known or generally overlooked material such as the manuscripts of Hardy's epitaphs on George Moore and G. K. Chesterton whose texts were first printed by J. O. Bailey in *The Poetry of Thomas Hardy* (1970) or Hardy's holograph comment on the conclusion to 'The Romantic Adventures of a Milkmaid' first printed by Michael Millgate in *Thomas Hardy: His Career as a Novelist* (1971). In such ways other textual materials have been uncovered or their significance reassessed, and, at the same time, manuscripts have changed hands, some relevant publishers' records have come to light – e.g., the Harper and Brothers records recently deposited in the Morgan Library and Columbia University Library – and still others have become more accessible, as is true of the important Macmillan papers sold to the British Museum in 1968.

In short, enough information is available, or potentially available, both corrective of and supplementary to Purdy's work, that the publication of a more nearly definitive descriptive bibliography would be desirable. In lieu of such a monumental undertaking, however, scholars would benefit greatly if some supplementary descriptive catalogues were made available: (1) of additions to and corrections of the Purdy bibliography; (2) of the Hardiana in the Dorset County Museum; (3) of Hardy's marginalia, including locations; and (4) of the reprintings of Hardy's works, both authorised and pirated, including information about the number and size of impressions and other data relevant to tracing the growth and changes of interest in Hardy's writings.

TEXTUAL ANALYSIS

The history of analytic studies of the revisions of Hardy's manuscripts and printed editions has been the subject of brief critical surveys by Dieter Riesner (*Archiv*, 1962) and R. C. Schweik (*English Literature in Transition*, 1971). Most of such analytic studies have focused on Hardy's fiction, and, apart from the work of J. W. Beach and Mary Ellen Chase already mentioned, the earliest analysis was that of the manuscript of *Two on a Tower* by Carl Weber (*Papers of the Bibliographical Society of America*, 1946). Weber plausibly accounted for textual differences between the manuscript and the first serial version by hypothesising the existence of a second copy with variant readings, part of which was subsequently incorporated in the manuscript now in the Houghton Library at Harvard. Although Weber's analysis is generally convincing, it was unfortunately marred by a serious misinterpretation of one part of the evidence, an error which remained unnoticed until pointed out some twenty years later by R. C. Schweik (*Papers of the Bibliographical Society of America*, 1966).

Weber's pioneering study was followed two years later by W. B. Bebbington's pamphlet-length account of the manuscript of *The Trumpet-Major* – really little more than an incomplete catalogue of revisions, prefaced by an entirely mistaken interpretation of the absence of revisions on manuscript leaves as signifying that Hardy wrote spontaneously and without alterations. Regrettably, a truly valuable analysis remains unpublished – Michael Edwards' M.A. thesis, 'The Making of Hardy's *The Trumpet-Major*' (University of Birmingham, 1967). Edwards shrewdly interprets the significance of Hardy's revisions (e.g., the way Hardy deliberately heightened class differences in the novel), he discusses the bowdlerising influence of editorial pressures on the novel, and he provides, in fact, a workmanlike study which should be published in some form.

The next novel to become the subject of any detailed textual study was *The Woodlanders*. In 'The Tragedy in Little Hintock' (*Booker Memorial Studies*, 1950), Carl Weber revealed dramatically what many critics from J. W. Beach onward had not suspected: the extraordinary weakness of some widely distributed American editions of the novel. Following upon this solid beginning, Dale Kramer published 'Revisions and Vision: Thomas Hardy's *The Woodlanders*' (*Bulletin of the New York Public Library*, 1971), a redaction of his 1963 Western Reserve doctoral dissertation. In it he traced and carefully interpreted the significance of textual changes in the novel from the manuscript through to the 'Wessex' edition and came to cautiously stated and generally reliable conclusions emphasising, particularly, that in the textual history of *The Woodlanders* very few of Hardy's major revisions seem to have been dictated by purely aesthetic considerations: the bulk of them, ranging from his efforts to clarify meanings to his gradually increasing frankness in treatment of sexual matters, Kramer showed to be in one way or another affected by external influences.

Dale Kramer's study of *The Woodlanders* had been preceded by R. C. Slack's 'The Text of Hardy's *Jude the Obscure*' (*Nineteenth Century Fiction*, 1957), based upon his research for a 1953 University of Pittsburgh doctoral dissertation. Slack revealed that Hardy had bowdlerised the 'pig's pizzle' episode when he revised for the 'Wessex' edition, and he also detailed the effect of other textual changes – e.g., those strongly affecting the characterisation of Sue Bridehead. Slack's brief comments on the manuscript of the novel in his dissertation had depended upon a microfilm copy and were scarcely revealing, and subsequently Hardy's manuscript revisions were discussed by John Paterson (*Studies in Philology*, 1960) in a study which strangely reached a conclusion exactly the reverse of what the manuscript evidence reveals. A more consistent interpretation of that evidence – that Hardy began *Jude* as a novel focused on sexual relationships and marriage, then later revised to stress Jude's scholastic ambitions – was suggested by R. C. Schweik (*English Literature in Transition*, 1971) and confirmed by Patricia Ingham's 'The Evolution of *Jude the Obscure*' (*Review of English Studies*, 1976), a splendidly astute analysis which established the complex relationship of the manuscript to the serial and first book editions (it affected both but was not the copy-text for either) and showed persuasively and in detail that Hardy's initial conception of the subject of the novel was the relationship of the sexes, to which only later and superficially did Hardy add the theme of frustrated academic aspiration.

The texts of *The Return of the Native* did not receive any detailed study until the publication of Otis Wheeler's 'Four Versions of *The Return of the Native*' (*Nineteenth Century Fiction*, 1959) which described Hardy's extensive revisions from the *Belgravia* serial version through the 'Wessex' edition. Wheeler argued that in later versions of the novel Hardy strengthened the main characters, tightened up the plot, and achieved a more direct and colloquial style; and he also called attention to some ways in which he thought Hardy's later revisions actually weakened the novel. Unfortunately, Wheeler's study was apparently prepared in ignorance of a 1954 University of Michigan doctoral dissertation which, in a revised form, was published as *The Making of the Return of the Native* in 1960. Paterson's much more extensive work included a study of the manuscript which had been ignored by Wheeler, and it is particularly notable for an argument that Hardy's manuscript contains traces of a much more sensational 'Ur-novel' in which, for example, Eustacia was presented as more than a metaphorical witch. In tracing the development of the novel through its printed editions, Paterson also pointed to Hardy's revisions in the role and character of Diggory Venn and to Hardy's efforts to make Clym a classical hero. Unfortunately, Paterson's study did not include all the relevant printed editions, and his interpretations of Hardy's revisions were sometimes ill-founded (as was the significance he attributed to Eustacia's hourglass), sometimes simply wrong (as was his assertion that the reddleman was originally Granfer Cantle's grandson), and often presented in an overstated way – so much so that the weaknesses of his argument became the subject of a penetrating critical analysis by Dieter Riesner (*Archiv*, 1963). More recently, F. B. Pinion (*TLS*, 1970) called attention to an unpublished letter by John Blackwood which not only makes it clear that Hardy had begun *The Return of the Native* earlier than had previously been suspected but also provides some insight into the difficulty Hardy had in finding a publisher for the novel in its earlier form.

The next of Hardy's texts to be given close study, *The Mayor of Casterbridge*, was the subject of Dieter Riesner's 'Kunstprosa in der Werkstatt' (*Festschrift für Walter Hübner*, 1964), a thorough and remarkably careful analysis of Hardy's revisions through six different versions from the 1884 manuscript to the Wessex text of 1912. Riesner touches on nearly every aspect of Hardy's alterations, from the most radical shifts in character and plot in the early portions of the manuscript to more subtle adjustments of tone and dialect in some later editions; and he constantly draws attention to the implications of these changes for literary criticism – pointing out, for example, that Hardy's revisions are not consistent with the 'sociological' emphasis which has been given to the novel by such scholars as Douglas Brown. However, in his consideration of the manuscript, Riesner did not attempt to identify different stages of revision by studying the relationship of Hardy's changes to the ink colours, pen styles, and paper stocks with which they may be associated. Subsequently, in 'The Manuscript of Hardy's *The Mayor of Casterbridge*' (*Papers of the Bibliographical Society of America*, 1973), Christine Winfield analysed the significance of such evidences, thus helpfully supplementing Riesner's study. But in doing so she unfortunately took no notice at all either of Riesner's work or of previously published studies of Hardy's first drafts and thus often simply repeated what had already been said.

The manuscript of *Tess of the d'Urbervilles* was first the subject of an article-length study (*AUMULA*, 1966) by John Laird, in which he discriminated some five 'layers' of manuscript draft largely on the basis of the evidence of name changes, and he was able to show conclusively that Hardy had revised much more heavily for the first book edition of *Tess* than Hardy's own account would have suggested. But Laird's interpretation of the significance of Hardy's revisions was in other respects strained, and his subsequent book-length analysis of Hardy's revisions (*The Shaping of Tess of the d'Urbervilles*, 1975) was also marred by dubious interpretations, mostly intended to emphasise the presence of an 'Ur-novel' in the manuscript. One weakness of Laird's analysis was his assumption that because certain matter appears on a manuscript leaf of a later 'layer' it must perforce have been a later conception; but, of course, there is often no way of telling whether, in fact, that matter may have existed in an earlier 'layer' and have been recopied: thus the fact that a third-'layer' leaf contains an authorial comment on nature's indifference is not, as Laird assumes (p. 75), evidence of Hardy's attempt to give greater prominence to this theme in later revisions. Similarly unreliable interpretations occur in Laird's discussion of changes in the printed texts of the novel. There is, for example, a passage in the *Graphic* printing of *Tess* which describes Clare's embracings of the heroine thus: 'Then he pressed her again to his side, for the unconstrained manners of Talbothays Dairy came convenient now.' In the first book version of *Tess*, Hardy revised that passage to include a description of how, after Tess 'had run her finger round the leads to cut off the cream edge', Angel Clare 'cleaned it in nature's way'. This addition, in which we are told that Clare sucks the cream from Tess's finger, is interpreted by Laird as an instance of Hardy's 'toning down of language describing Angel's embracings of the heroine' (p. 163) when, clearly, it does the reverse by adding an additional sensual and erotic element to a passage otherwise unchanged. Unfortunately, then, a thoroughly convincing interpretation of the significance of Hardy's revisions of *Tess* remains to be published.

Far from the Madding Crowd was the last of Hardy's novels to receive any detailed textual study, and that only a limited analysis of the manuscript by R. C. Schweik (*Texas Studies in Literature and Language*, 1967) which argues that at first Hardy probably did not plan to dramatise the stories of either Boldwood or Fanny Robin. Subsequently, there were very brief studies of an extant first-draft chapter of the novel, one by Clarice Short (*Bulletin of the Rocky Mountain MLA*, 1971) and another by R. C. Schweik (*English Studies*, 1972), both calling attention to a self-borrowing by Hardy, and the latter suggesting that a phrasing of Oak's speech in the first draft implied that in an early state of the development of the story Oak was probably not an independent farmer but Bathsheba's shepherd.

Apart from the textual studies of Hardy's fiction described above, little else has been done in the fifty years since his death. On the short stories, for example, there has been only Evelyn Hardy's slight 'Plots for Five Unpublished Short Stories' (*London Magazine*, 1958), which reproduces five summary-plots possibly not for short stories at all, and Alistair McLeod's unpublished dissertation (Notre Dame, 1969) which examines Hardy's revisions in *A Group of Noble Dames* and speculates, not entirely convincingly, on the effect of editorial pressures on the later forms of the stories. There have been two studies of Hardy's illustrators, one by Norman Page (*Bulletin of the New York Public Library*, 1974) and another, an unpublished doctoral dissertation by Robert F. Kaufman (New York University, 1974). Astonishingly, until very recently, practically no interest has been taken in the history of Hardy's revisions of his poems. In 1969 Kenneth Marsden devoted one chapter of his *The Poems of Thomas Hardy* to a study of Hardy's revisions of *Wessex Poems* and came to a necessarily very tentative conclusion that they exhibit a 'curve' of revision, first toward greater oddness and idiosyncrasy of diction and syntax, and then away from it; a similar tendency of Hardy's revisions to be in the direction of greater oddity was noted by Walter Wright in his *The Shaping of 'The Dynasts'* (1967). And, finally, in a chapter in *Thomas Hardy and the Modern World* (1974), James Gibson traced the main published editions of Hardy's poems, stressed the textual importance of the manuscripts, and called for a modern edition of Hardy's writings.

Such, then, is the history of analytic studies of Hardy's texts in the last fifty years. That so many of them are seriously flawed, unconvincing, and far from exhaustive suggests, of course, that all too often they have been prepared without sufficient caution, without a sense of the full complexity of the evidence, and perhaps without an adequate appreciation of the value of thoroughness. But it should be added at once that even the most elaborately full of the studies described above are all radically incomplete: the evidences they present are invariably selected, and the selection does not allow a reader to consider the total body of data from which the evidence was taken and which even the most careful selection may subtly distort. The fact is that analytic studies simply cannot satisfactorily serve as substitutes for direct consideration of the textual evidence itself, any more than a critical study of a novel can satisfactorily serve as a substitute for the novel itself. What a fully informed Hardy scholarship requires, then, is critical editions which provide both authoritative texts and full records of all textual variants so that each scholar and critic may see for himself what editorial choices have been made and interpret for himself the significance of Hardy's revisions. And this brings us to consider the history of the editing of Hardy's texts.

EDITING

In talking about editing it is useful to distinguish between 'practical' and 'critical' editions. Good practical editions are usually achieved by faithfully following some well-accepted text – 'the last edition overseen by the author in his lifetime', 'the text declared by the author to embody his final intention', or the like. In Hardy's case this is the 1912 Macmillan 'Wessex' edition. Thanks to Richard L. Purdy's authoritative assertion that 'the Wessex Edition is in every sense the definitive edition of Hardy's work' and thanks also to Carl Weber's warnings about the defects of American editions, the preparation of modern practical editions of Hardy's writings proceeds on a sounder footing. Many such editions now include some assurance that the text presented follows the 'Wessex' edition; some – e.g., the Norton Critical edition – include limited textual notes and sometimes textual analysis as well; and one, an edition of *Jude the Obscure* by Frank Southerington, provides more than usually extensive textual notes and even ventures (quite rightly, I believe) to emend the 'Wessex' text by substituting the less bowdlerised version of the 'pig's pizzle' episode printed in 1895. But with this exception and a few editions of *Far from the Madding Crowd* which incorporate a minor emendation, such practical editions simply follow more or less faithfully, but uncritically, one or another of the impressions of the

'Wessex' edition. Later impressions of the 'Wessex' edition, incorporating revisions Hardy made after the publication of the 'Mellstock' edition in 1918, were formerly available in the 'Library' or 'Greenwood' texts but have now gone out of print, and Macmillan of London are now publishing a 'New Wessex Edition', completely reset by film process. For the most part this edition uncritically follows the original 'Wessex' text, with, of course, the inevitable intrusion of compositorial error; but the 'New Wessex Edition' is, nevertheless, certainly the most important practical edition of Hardy's work ever undertaken: when completed it will make available for the first time nearly the entire canon of Hardy's published writings, including previously uncollected texts in the volumes edited by James Gibson (the poems) and by F. B. Pinion (the short stories); and Gibson's edition includes exceptionally valuable, though by no means complete, textual notes. Furthermore, the 'New Wessex Edition' is being published in both hardback and paperback forms, the latter especially attractive for classroom use because, although the 'New Wessex' texts have very uneven introductions, the explanatory notes they provide are exceptionally good. Users should be warned that the hardback and paperback impressions of the 'New Wessex' have different paginations and that, consequently, references to this edition must specify the binding. For scholarly purposes the 'Wessex' edition of 1912 will remain the standard reference text until such time as critical editions become available.

And critical editions are very much needed, for, of course, the 'Wessex' edition is far from 'the definitive edition of Hardy's work'; it is, in fact, a corrupt text, the product of a long history of corruption which began with Hardy's own oversights in drafting his manuscripts, followed by further corruptions which came about as the result of compositorial error and editorial intrusion, and including Hardy's self-bowdlerisations, both early and late, in acquiescence to public pressures. It is the purpose of editors of critical editions to provide texts – based on all the available evidence from manuscripts, proof copy, printed editions, unprinted revises, publishers' records, and the like – which will eliminate these corruptions and represent, as fully and accurately as possible, Hardy's final deliberate authorial intention. Hardy's writings pose some awkward problems for editors preparing such editions. The manuscripts, for example, are, when extant, not always complete, and some portions of them are in the first Mrs Hardy's hand and are, thus, questionable as witnesses of Hardy's intention; and there is not yet any clear agreement on what tests discriminate between the two hands – see, for example, Carl Weber (1946) and Dale Kramer (1963), both in *Papers of the Bibliographical Society of America*, and Robert Gittings in *TLS* (1962).

Hence, of course, even the most careful of critical editions will provide a text which, although authoritative, will be the product of fallible editorial judgement and certainly not 'definitive' in any absolute sense; but because such editions also provide the reader with a description and history of the texts, lists of all substantive and accidental variants, and a detailed statement of the principles and practices adopted by the editor, each user may interpret for himself the textual evidences and need not depend upon the editor's judgement. What is important to emphasise here is that such editions are the *sine qua non* both of well founded critical judgements and fully informed historical interpretations of Hardy's work.

It goes without saying that such editions must above all be both exhaustively thorough and scrupulously accurate, and, as the early volumes of the ill-fated Ohio edition of Browning all too clearly show, they may be neither. So far only one attempt at a critical edition of Hardy's writings has been published in any form – a microfilmed edition of *The Woodlanders* prepared as a doctoral dissertation by Marilyn Hubbart (University of Nebraska, 1971). It includes a very interesting critical discussion of the novel and much valuable information on the revisions of its texts, but unfortunately it is neither acceptably thorough nor unquestionably accurate : the editor did not take into consideration the very important evidence of Hardy's holograph revisions in his copy of the 1906 Macmillan printing which was used as a copy-text for the 'Wessex' edition and is now in the Dorset County Museum;[1] nor does she consider the detailed analysis of the texts available in Dale Kramer's 1963 Western Reserve doctoral dissertation; and a check of only a few selected leaves for accuracy revealed some five cases where accidentals differed from those in the copy-text without explanation and turned up at least one unexplained substantive variant as well. In short, fifty years after Hardy's death not one of the works printed in his lifetime has yet been published in a critical edition done to the highest modern standards.

Fortunately, this state of affairs is about to be corrected. Some splendidly done critical editions of Hardy's works do exist in unpublished form – for example, Simon Gatrell's critical edition of *Under the Greenwood Tree*, an unpublished Oxford doctoral dissertation (1973) which is a work of modern critical editing done to the very highest standards. The Clarendon Press is now preparing to publish Juliet Grindle's critical edition of *Tess of the d'Urbervilles*, and there are plans to continue with other critical editions of some of the novels and the poetry. There is every reason to believe that these editions will probably surpass the high standard set by the critical editions of some works of Dickens and the Brontës which have already appeared under the Clarendon Press imprint. One can only hope that Clarendon will continue the series to something like completeness, including not only the poetry and the fiction but also such works as Hardy's autobiography, published under Florence Emily Hardy's name but written almost entirely by him.

As pressing as has been the need for scholarly critical editions of those works of Hardy's which he published during his lifetime, there has been an even greater need for editions of his letters and notebooks, access to which has long been one of the greatest difficulties of Hardy scholarship. What remains of Hardy's correspondence is widely scattered, and some of it is in the form of rough drafts only. What has been published during the fifty years since Hardy's death has left a mare's nest of multiple, incomplete editions, checklists, brief notes, and incidental printings of individual letters in whole or in part. The chief editions have been three: Carl Weber's *The Letters of Thomas Hardy* (1954), which in fact only includes letters in the Colby College Library; *Dearest Emmie* (1963), Hardy's letters to his first wife, also edited by Weber; and Evelyn Hardy and F. B. Pinion's *One Rare Fair Woman* (1972), which provides the Hardy–Henniker correspondence. These editions all include introductions and very useful notes. Of great value, although weakened by inaccuracies, is Carl and Clara Weber's *Thomas Hardy's Correspondence at Max Gate* (1968), which catalogues letters by Hardy and by others to Hardy now in the Dorset County Museum, and Richard Cary's calendar of letters from, to, and about Hardy in the Colby College collection (*Colby Library Quarterly*, 1971). Other letters have been published under a wide variety of circumstances. Some appeared during Hardy's lifetime as replies to critics, explanations, and the like. A. Edward Newton printed a facsimile of a Hardy–Tinsley letter in the *Atlantic Monthly* as early as 1915. After Hardy's death other letters continued to appear, sometimes singly, sometimes in groups, sometimes only partially or inaccurately. Purdy's *Thomas Hardy: A Bibliographical Study* included a calendar of the Hardy–Tinsley letters and texts of six letters of Leslie Stephen to Hardy; three letters to Henry James from Hardy (out of a total of some sixty Hardy letters now at Harvard) were provided by Carl Weber's 'Hardy and James' (*Harvard Library Bulletin*, 1968); Carl Ziegler's 'Thomas Hardy's Correspondence with German Translators' (*English Literature in Transition*, 1968) describes Hardy's draft responses to requests from German publishers; and there have been many shorter publications with such titles as 'An Unpublished Hardy Letter', 'Thomas Hardy in 1916: A New Letter', and so forth. Any catalogue of the output of such printings would be quite impossible here, and, fortunately, it will soon be unnecessary: the Clarendon Press now plans to publish a collected edition of Hardy's letters, prepared by Richard L. Purdy and Michael Millgate, the first volume of which is scheduled to appear in 1978 or shortly after. When this edition is completed, scholars will have access for the first time to a full and reliable scholarly edition of Hardy's letters.

At the same time progress is being made in the editing of that small number of Hardy's personal notebooks and scrapbooks which survive, most of them in the Dorset County Museum. These are of potentially great value for what they can reveal about Hardy's thought and art, and they deserve editing. The editions which have appeared so far vary widely in quality: Evelyn Hardy's *Thomas Hardy's Notebooks* (1955), an edition of notebooks titled 'Memoranda' (I and II), was both incomplete and inaccurate; on the other hand, C. J. P. Beatty's *The Architectural Notebook of Thomas Hardy* (1966) and Lennart Björk's *The Literary Notes of Thomas Hardy* (Volume I, 1974) are both models of textual accuracy and include exceptionally illuminating notes. G. Stevens Cox's transcription of Hardy's *Trumpet-Major Notebook* was spread over three issues of the *Thomas Hardy Yearbook* (1971, 1972–3, and 1973–4) and is in this and other respects unsatisfactory. Fortunately, those notebooks printed in the editions by Evelyn Hardy and J. Stevens Cox will be edited again, along with the remaining unedited notebooks, by Richard H. Taylor, and it is thus likely that in the near future satisfactory editions of all the extant notebooks not in private hands will be available to scholars.

Some mention should be made here, too, of the eighteen reels of microfilm of Hardy manuscripts in the Dorset County Museum and elsewhere in England which were published in 1976 by EP Microform Ltd; these include not only the notebooks and commonplace books but such things as the typescript of the *Life* and, of course, the manuscripts of many of the major novels and poems. Such an edition has, however, only very limited scholarly value; manuscript evidences so often turn on such matters as ink colour, paper stock, traces of erasure, and the like, that any study of microfilm copies is likely to be an exercise in futility. Much more useful would be an edition of some of Hardy's very minor essays and reminiscences which are very difficult to obtain. Some of these were collected by Ernest Brennecke in an edition titled *Life and Art* (1925), now long out of print; more recently, Harold Orel has edited a collection titled *Thomas Hardy's Personal Writings* (1966) which provides nearly twice as much material as Brennecke. Unfortunately, however, Orel did not publish the earlier versions of Hardy's prefaces, nor did he take the desirable course of reprinting all of the minor writings. Orel did, however, summarise those texts he felt were too trivial to publish, and in this way he supplemented some of the briefer annotations already available in Purdy's *Thomas Hardy: A Descriptive Bibliography*. It is likely that even these remaining minor writings will be published reasonably soon.

CONCLUSION

In short, although an account of the study of Hardy's texts over the last fifty years must be largely a history of preliminary work and disappointingly fragmented scholarship, much of it of very limited value, the time is now at hand when that history of neglect is finally being remedied. With the ongoing publication of practical editions of good quality, including the extensive 'New Wessex' edition by Macmillan; with well advanced plans by the Clarendon Press for publication of scholarly critical editions of the poems, the letters, and at least some of the fiction; and with a high probability that the remaining notebooks will be satisfactorily edited – there are signs that what has been sown during the first fifty years of textual scholarship on Hardy is finally bearing fruit.

NOTES

1   I am indebted to Professor Dale Kramer for first calling my attention to the existence of this copy-text in the Dorset County Museum.

Index

Aeschylus, 1, 2, 4, 23
Aristotle, 16
Arnold, Matthew, 1, 2, 3, 12, 24,
   61, 111, 112
Auden, W. H., 63
Austen, Jane, 2, 26

Bab, Howard, 136
Bailey, J. O., 47, 137
Balzac, Honoré, 78, 79
Barnes, William, 50
Barthes, Roland, 79
Beach, J. W., 135, 139
Beatty, C. J. P., 147
Bebbington, W. B., 138
Beckett, Samuel, 118, 119
Betjeman, John, 63
Bible, The, 5, 6, 23, 50
Björk, L., 147
Botticelli, 97
Britten, Benjamin, 73
Brontës, The, 145
Brennecke, Ernest, 147
Brown, Douglas, 141
Browning, Robert, 9, 44, 52, 55,
   145
Byron, Lord, 1

Cary, Richard, 146
Camus, Albert, 24
Chase, Mary Ellen, 135
Chaucer, Geoffrey, 134
Chekhov, Anton, 59
Chesterton, G. K., 47, 137
Colenso, Bishop, 68
Comte, Auguste, 3, 127
Conrad, Joseph, 26, 74, 117
Correggio, 98
Cox, G. Stevens, 147
Crabbe, George, 53

Danielson, H., 137
Dante, 116, 117, 122

Darwin, Charles, 64, 65, 66, 67, 127
Davie, Donald, 59, 63
Day-Lewis, C., 126
Dickens, Charles, 24, 116, 117, 118,
   122, 145
Drummond, Henry, 64
Dürer, Albrecht, 97

Edel, Leon, 78, 79
Edwards, Michael, 138
Eliot, George, 15, 23, 24, 26, 117,
   118, 119, 120, 121
Eliot, T. S., 6, 43, 46, 49, 52, 53,
   55, 59, 66, 67, 75, 91
Essays and Reviews, 65
Euripides, 23

Ferrey, Benjamin, 9
Ford, Ford Maddox, 50, 51, 52
Fowles, John, 31, 35, 38
France, Anatole, 16
Freud, Sigmund, 23

Gattrell, Simon, 145
Gibson, James, 142, 144
Gide, André, 24
Gifford, Emma, 39, 72, 128, 132,
   133, 144; see also Hardy,
   Emma
Gittings, Robert, 144
Goethe, 1, 7
Gosse, Edmund, 43, 48, 51, 129, 130
Graves, Robert, 63
Gray, Thomas, 50, 61
Grindle, Juliet, 145
Guerard, A. J., 135, 136

Hafiz, 116
Hardy, Emma, 34, 44, 45, 55, 70,
   71, 76; see also Gifford,
   Emma
Hardy, Evelyn, 47, 142, 146

Hardy, Thomas,
  'Absolute Explains, The', 76
  'According to the Mighty Work-
    ing', 8
  'After a Journey', 55, 56, 57, 58,
    59
  'After the Fair', 10
  'Afterwards', 8, 10, 60, 61, 62, 63
  'Ancient to Ancients, An', 51, 134
  'Aquae Sulis', 10
  'At a Bridal', 69
  'At Castle Boterel', 52, 56
  'At Rushy Pond', 45
  'August Midnight, An', 8, 54, 57
  'Beeny Cliff', 58, 60
  'Before Life and After', 73
  'Before my Friend Arrived', 45
  'Blinded Bird, The', 48
  Boldwood (*Far From the Mad-
    ding Crowd*), 40, 120, 142
  Bridehead, Sue, 4, 100, 101, 114,
    115, 121, 123, 131, 139
  Charmond, Mrs, 87
  'Christmas in the Elgin Room', 10
  Clare, Angel, 20, 21, 99, 100,
    111, 112, 121, 141
  'Clasped Skeletons, The', 10
  'Coronation, The', 10
  'Darkling Thrush, The', 8, 62, 132
  'Dead Man Walking, The', 45
  Desperate Remedies, 4, 19, 29, 33,
    51, 72, 104, 105, 106, 107, 108,
    109, 127, 128, 129
  'Discouragement', 8
  'Domicilium', 53
  Donn, Arabella, 34, 99, 100, 121,
    122
  'Dream-Follower, The', 10
  'Drummer Hodge', 8, 132
  d'Urberville, Alec, 99, 100, 121
  Durbeyfield, Tess, 4, 5, 7, 8, 20,
    21, 35, 51, 57, 74, 80, 99,
    100, 111, 121, 130, 132, 134,
    136, 141
  'During Wind and Rain', 48
  Dynasts, The, 3, 5, 8, 13, 50, 51,
    59, 69, 75, 119, 124, 131, 132,
    134
  Egdon Heath, 4, 8, 25, 57, 59, 80,
    81, 84, 85, 93, 112, 132
  'Evening Shadows', 11
  Everdene, Bathsheba, 4, 6, 7, 120,
    129, 142

'Experience, An', 45
Farfrae, Donald, 111, 121
Far From the Madding Crowd, 7,
  9, 15, 39, 61, 110, 120, 125, 129,
  136, 142, 143
Fawley, Jude, 6, 51, 74, 109, 114,
  115, 121, 123, 127, 131
Fitzpiers, Edred, 80, 86, 87, 112,
  121
'Five Students, The', 48
'Friends Beyond', 132
'God's Funeral', 69
'Going, The', 52
Group of Noble Dames, A, 10,
  142
'Had You Wept', 45
Hand of Ethelberta, The, 19, 129
'Hap', 65, 69, 71, 127
'Head Above the Fog, The', 48
Henchard (Newson), Elizabeth-
  Jane, 6, 121
Henchard, Michael, 8, 111, 121,
  123, 130, 132, 134
'He Never Expected Much', 72
'He Resolves to Say No More', 5
'He, to Her', 55
'House of Silence, The', 11
'I Look into my Glass', 113
'Impercipient, The', 132
'In a Museum', 8
*Indiscretion in the Life of an
  Heiress, An*, 29, 36, 87
'Interloper, The', 48
'In the Seventies', 45, 48
'In Vision I Roamed', 69
'John and Jane', 8
Jude the Obscure, 9, 16, 23, 30,
  34, 38, 47, 48, 49, 59, 61, 65,
  75, 78, 95, 99, 101, 102, 104,
  114, 115, 121, 122, 123, 125,
  131, 134, 139, 143
'Just the Same', 4
'Kiss, A', 8
Knight, Henry, 4, 17, 18, 56, 106,
  128
Laodicean, A, 20, 129
Late Lyrics and Earlier, 53, 68
'Life and Death at Sunrise', 4
Life of Thomas Hardy, The, 12, 13,
  14, 69, 70, 74, 105, 106, 109,
  120, 147
Little Father Time, 4, 59, 115

Mayor of Casterbridge, The, 6, 8, 23, 95, 101, 120, 130, 140
Melbury, Grace, 80, 86, 87, 111, 121
Melbury, Mr., 111
'Midnight on the Great Western', 47, 48
'Moments of Vision', 10, 47
'Near Lanivet, 1872', 39, 48
'Neutral Tones', 1, 45, 47
'1967', 69
Notebooks of Thomas Hardy, The, 147
Oak, Gabriel, 53, 57, 120, 129, 142
'Old Mrs. Chundle', 5
'On a Heath', 45, 48
'Opportunity, The', 9
'Oxen, The', 48
Pair of Blue Eyes, A, 16, 17, 56, 57, 106, 109, 128
'Pedigree, The', 8
Phillotson, Mr., 121, 122
Pierston, Jocelyn, 4, 22, 29, 32, 34, 37, 39, 40, 112, 113, 114
'Pity of it, The', 133
'Plaint to Man, A', 133
Poems 1912–1913, 49, 52, 53, 55, 56, 70, 71
Poems of the Past and the Present, 132
Poor Man and the Lady, The, 24, 72, 87, 127, 128
'Procession of Dead Days, A', 44
'Profitable Reading of Fiction, The', 2
Queen of Cornwall, The Famous Tragedy of, 16
Return of the Native, The, 6, 16, 20, 80, 81, 82, 83, 84, 85, 87, 92, 93, 107, 111, 112, 120, 129, 140
Robin, Fanny, 5, 142
'Romantic Adventures of a Milkmaid, The', 137
Satires of Circumstance, 133
'Self-Unseeing, The', 132
'She Hears the Storm', 9
'She, to Him', 1, 4, 55
'She Visits Alone the Church of her Marriage', 8
'So, Time', 76
South, Marty, 86, 121

Stonehenge, 22
Talbothays, 7, 8, 74, 111, 119
'Temporary the All, The', 10
Tess of the d'Urbervilles, 4, 6, 17, 21, 43, 80, 95, 99, 101, 121, 124, 130, 131, 135, 141, 142, 145
'Thoughts of Phena', 131
'Thunderstorm in Town, A', 133
Troy, Sgt., 4, 6, 120
Trumpet-Major, The, 129, 132, 138
Two on a Tower, 3, 10, 57, 130
'Two Roses', 46
Under the Greenwood Tree, 9, 23, 128, 145
'Under the Waterfall', 60
Venn, Diggory, 83, 84, 93, 120, 140
'Voices from Things Growing in a Churchyard', 8
Vye, Eustacia, 4, 7, 17, 20, 21, 45, 80, 83, 84, 85, 93, 120, 140
'Waiting Both', 11
'Waiting Supper, The', 9
'Waterfall, The', 52
'We Are Getting to the End', 5
'We Sat at the Window', 70, 72
Weatherbury, 111
'We Five', 55
Well-Beloved, The, 12, 22, 24, 29, 30, 32, 33, 34, 36, 37, 38, 40, 104, 106, 112, 113, 114, 131
'Wessex Heights', 46
Wessex Poems, 53, 131, 142
'When I Set out for Lyonnesse', 133
Wildeve, Damon, 80, 83, 84, 85, 120
'Wind Blew Words, The', 8
Winterborne, Giles, 86, 87, 111, 121, 130
Woodlanders, The, 2, 9, 74, 80, 86, 87, 121, 130, 135, 139, 145
Yeobright, Clym, 4, 7, 17, 20, 21, 22, 23, 24, 45, 80, 85, 93, 111, 112, 120, 129, 140
Yeobright, Mrs., 4, 83, 84, 120
Yeobright, Thomasin, 93, 120
'Young Man's Epigram on Existence', 69
Harrison, F., 5
Herbert, George, 116
Hopkins, G. M., 58, 65, 66
Hughes, Ted, 49

Hubbart, Marilyn, 145
Hugo, Victor, 6
Huxley, T. H., 68, 127

Ibsen, Henrik, 59

Jakobson, R., 78, 79
James, Henry, 15, 24, 26, 43, 49, 146
Johnson, Samuel, 61
Joyce, James, 24, 79

Keats, John, 8
Kierkegaard, Søren, 24, 67
Kingsley, Charles, 68
Kramer, Dale, 137, 139, 144, 145

Lack, David, 68
Laird, John, 141
Lane, John, 137
Larkin, Philip, 63
Lawrence, D. H., 59, 63, 75, 90ff
Lea, Herman, 126
Leavis, F. R., 49

Macleod, Alastair, 142
Mann, Thomas, 24
Marsden, Kenneth, 142
Marx, Karl, 24
Maurice, F. D., 68
Michelangelo, 97
Mill, J. S., 3, 127
Miller, J. Hillis, 82
Millgate, Michael, 137, 147
Milton, John, 7, 61, 73, 75
Monod, Prof. J., 64
Moore, George, 47, 137
Morgan, Charles, 13, 25
Moule, Horace, 40, 45, 127
Murdoch, Iris, 109
Murry, John Middleton, 4

Newman, Cardinal, 63, 119
Newton, A. E., 146

Omar Khayyam, 3, 75
Orel, Harold, 147

Page, Norman, 142
Pater, Walter, 1, 3, 11, 12
Paterson, John, 139, 140
Paterson, Helen, 9
Phelps, Prof. W. L., 43

Pinion, F. B., 140, 144, 146
Poems and Ballads, 65
Pound, Ezra, 49, 51, 52, 53, 59, 60, 63
Proust, Marcel, 24
Purdy, R. L., 46, 48, 137, 143, 146, 147, 148

Raphael, 97
Reichard, H. M., 136
Rembrandt, 98
Richardson, Samuel, 6
Riesner, Dieter, 138, 140, 141
Rose, Prof. Gilbert J., 31, 38
Ruskin, John, 23

Schweik, R. C., 136, 138, 139, 142
Schweitzer, Albert, 67
Shakespeare, William, 1, 2, 4, 6, 7, 15, 18, 23, 50, 57, 58, 74, 93, 95, 116, 117, 118, 119, 122, 128, 134
Shelley, Percy Bysshe, 3, 132
'Shepheardes Calendar, The', 110
Shirley, James, 7
Short, Clarice, 142
Slack, R. C., 139
Sophocles, 1, 6, 23, 74, 93
Southerington, Frank, 143
Sparks, Tryphena, 38, 39, 40, 127, 128, 129, 131, 132
Spiritual Exercises (Ignatius Loyola), 66
Stephen, Leslie, 1, 24, 70, 131, 146
Stevens, Wallace, 23
Stevenson, R. L., 43
Swinburne, Algernon Charles, 4, 127

Taylor, R. H., 147
Tennyson, Alfred, Lord, 64, 65
Tolstoy, Leo, 67, 79, 93
Trollope, Anthony, 24
Turner, J. M. W., 98, 130
Tyndall, Prof., 69

Van Ghent, D., 135, 136
Virgil, 55, 56, 60

Webb, A. P., 137
Weber, Carl, 136, 138, 139, 143, 144, 146
Wells, H. G., 30
Wheeler, Otis, 140
Whitman, Walt, 50, 52

Williams, W. C., 23
Winfield, Christine, 140
Woolf, Virginia, 13
Wordsworth, William, 1, 2, 44, 50,
    52, 53, 54, 55, 59, 60, 61

Wright, Walter, 142

Yeats, W. B., 47, 49, 54, 59

Ziegler, Carl, 146